I'm Counting to 10 . . .

I'm Counting to 10 . . .

Hope and Humor for Frazzled Parents

Jahnna Beecham and Malcolm Hillgartner

Featured columnists in *Sesame Street Parents* magazine

 SORIN BOOKS   Notre Dame, IN

International Standard Book Number: 1-893732-25-8

Cover, text design and illustrations by Katherine Robinson Coleman

Printed and bound in the United States of America.

Library of Congress Cataloging-in-Publication Data

Beecham, Jahnna.
    I'm counting to 10—:hope and humor for frazzled parents / Jahnna Beecham and Malcolm Hillgartner.
        p. cm.
    A collection of reflections originally published in Sesame Street parents magazine.
        ISBN 1-893732-25-8 (pbk.)
        1. Parenting—Humor. 2. Parenthood—Humor. I. Title: I am counting to ten—. II. Hillgartner, Malcolm. III. Title.

PN6231.P2 B44 2001
814'.54—dc21
                                                                00—11677
                                                                   CIP

For Bob

Our good friend and editor,
who wouldn't let us use the title we wanted:

"Who Are These Children and
Why Are They Calling Me Mom?"

ontents

Welcome to the Club

Malcolm and I want to make one thing perfectly clear. Parenthood took us completely by surprise. We had no intention of having children. We had a great life. Why ruin it? After ten years of marriage without kids, our friends found it extremely amusing that we wound up having not one, but two children. Do you remember those, "Oh, no, I left the baby on the bus!" tee shirts? We were barraged with them. Then, before we could say, "Push!" we joined the We-Never-Sleep parents club. Suddenly we had a minivan littered with Happy Meal containers, melted crayons and discarded clothing items. (We're past the baby stage, but we still have the suspicion that a bottle of curdled milk lurks somewhere under the back seat.)

In those early sleep-deprived days we felt very isolated. We lived way out in the country with our baby daughter Skye, the barf-and-poop machine, and son Dash, poster child for the Terrible Twos. None of our friends had children. And they wanted nothing to do with ours. Every invitation started with, "Can you get a sitter?" We felt like the loneliest people on the planet.

It wasn't until we vacationed at a family camp that we realized we weren't the only lepers in this colony. I sat around the pool in my floor-length bathing suit with reinforced underwire bra talking to other mothers in the same outfit. We discussed toilet training and time-out. It was like someone opened a window and let in the light. We weren't terrible parents! Everyone's kids threw tantrums in grocery stores, ran up and down the aisles on planes, and tried to poke their baby sister's eye out. We had found our club!

Shortly after that, we moved to a small town in Oregon filled with kids, dogs, playgrounds—and friends. Friends who, like us, haven't read a real book in years. They can sometimes be found behind the wheel at the school's "hug and go," still wearing their pajamas. And they are really patient when you call them on the phone and interrupt the conversation every two minutes to yell at your kids.

Basically, this book is to let you know that you are not alone. We're all in this club together. And in our club there are some universal truths: No two kids are alike. There isn't one right way to be a parent. If you can't figure it out, consult the experts . . . and most of the real experts don't have Ph.D. attached to their name. Their professional titles are "Mommy" or "Daddy." They are next door, or a phone call away in Denver, Minneapolis, South Bend, or Cleveland.

Who's Been Sleeping in My Bed?

Last night I heard a noise, leapt out of bed, and slammed into a wall. I bruised my nose and was certain I'd gone blind. I wouldn't have hit that wall if I'd been in my own bed. But I was in Dash's bed. Not with Dash. Dash was in my bed with Skye. And Malcolm had collapsed in Skye's bed.

We don't start the night that way. But sometime around 1:30 a.m. a silent alarm goes off. Dash races into our room, steps on the dog, and falls into bed with us. Twenty minutes later Skye shrieks, "Mommy! I'm scared!" I leap up, step on the dog, and race to her room. I escort Skye away from the Big Hairy Thing lurking in her open closet. We go to the bathroom, get a drink of water, and then she insists on going to sleep in the "Big Bed." Why children call it the Big Bed I'll never know. When all four of us are smushed into ours, it's definitely the smallest bed in the house.

Now, I know the habit of letting your children sleep with you is one of those dark secrets that no parent ever discloses. But I assure you, there are more kids who sleep with their parents than those who don't.

In the early days it was comforting to have the kids snuggled in with us. Dash would go to sleep holding Malcolm's hand. I would fall asleep with Skye's head nuzzled under my chin. Then came the squirming, hitting, and kicking period. One night Dash whapped me so hard in the eye, I saw stars. Malcolm has been kicked so many times in the crotch he sleeps on his stomach. Now we dream of a time when we'll be all alone. We say things like, "Surely children don't sleep with their parents when they're in junior high?"

There are several ways to stop all of this stumbling-around-in-the-night nonsense. There's the Cold Turkey approach: Lock your door and wear earplugs. (I have a friend whose son sleeps in a sleeping bag outside their locked door.) The Compromise (favored by many): Have your child sleep in a sleeping bag on the floor beside your bed. Or the Bribe: When we first moved to Oregon, a friend told us she was paying her son twenty-five cents a night to stay out of her bed. Now, two years later, that kid has gotten a raise. He's up to a dollar!

When we lived in Montana, we tried our own version of weaning Dash and Skye away from our bed: we moved their beds into our bedroom. Malcolm and I had the Big Bed. Dash was in his twin bed on Malcolm's side. And Skye slept in her toddler bed next to me. We figured we'd just keep moving their beds farther away until at last they'd be sleeping soundly in their own rooms. We never got that far. When we decided to sell our house, our realtor said, "You have got to do something about your bedroom. It's too weird. People think the Three Bears live here."

A non-parent friend I know just shakes her head in disgust and mutters, "Boundaries. You have to set boundaries." She's right, of course. But how can you set boundaries when it's two in the morning and you haven't had a good night's sleep in seven years? I know, I know. We've made our bed and we should lie in it. We'd like to—but there's no room!

Losing It

It's a fact that once you become a parent, you lose your hearing. This comes with the territory. (Like weight with marriage. Malcolm said, "I do," I said, "I do, too," and we instantly gained ten pounds.)

I remember the exact moment we went deaf. We were sitting in a restaurant talking to a non-parent friend. After about twenty minutes of pleasant conversation, our friend turned to us with a pained look on her face and said, "Does he have to do that?" Dash was beside us in his high chair, merrily hammering away at the metal tray with a spoon. We hadn't heard a thing. Why? Because he wasn't crying. And crying is the only sound that matters. Pounding the piano, kicking the back of your car seat, singing the alphabet song over and over—these are happy sounds that mean you can finish your meal, read the newspaper, or even balance your checkbook.

But your hearing isn't all that disintegrates after you have a child. Your dignity crumbles, too. Mine went first. Malcolm would sniff the air and whisper, "Do you think Dash needs a diaper change?" It didn't matter where we were—a fancy restaurant, a chic boutique, an elegant gathering. I'd lift Dash up, smash my face into his bottom, and announce, "Whoo-ee! It's ripe in there!"

In the early days, though flabby and deaf, we still had moments of lucidity. When Dash threw a tantrum at the check-out stand because his dad wouldn't buy him another Lego, Malcolm's face would blaze red. That was appropriate. And when Skye wailed from her perch in the grocery cart, "I want my Mommy!" I would start to sweat and announce to anyone in ear shot, "I am the Mommy! She's just joking." That, too, was appropriate.

Then something snapped. Along with our hearing and dignity, we lost our minds. It happened to me one morning at Safeway.

I had barely grabbed a grocery cart when the children began fighting over who would ride in the basket and who would ride on the shelf below. Normally, I would have shouted, "Stop that right now!" and tossed in a few threats about putting them in the car and going straight home. But on this particular day, I let them go at it. As they screamed, I stared vacantly into space and thought, "These aren't my children. I'm not their mother. I'm not even here. Some other body is pushing this cart. The real me is completely invisible." I wheeled the cart to the cereal section, where the children demanded I buy boxes of Fruit Loops and Sugar Pops. I smiled, nodded, and reached for the bran flakes, then pushed on. They raced after me, struggling to get into the moving cart, shouting, "Mom, what's the matter with you? Don't you see us?"

That was my first out-of-body experience. Now I use it all the time. So does Malcolm. In shopping malls. In the car. We even use it with each other. In fact, I'm using it now. You see, I'm not really sitting at my computer, surrounded by piles of laundry and screaming children. I'm in Bermuda, wearing my string bikini, and sipping a daiquiri.

The P Word

Before Malcolm and I had children, we didn't spend a whole lot of time talking about bodily functions. Maybe with relatives. Not with friends. And certainly not with strangers. Now a day doesn't go by that we don't discuss poop.

It all starts with your newborn's first diaper change. You undo the Pamper flaps and your spouse rushes into the room. "Did he poop yet?" "Not yet." A day goes by. Nothing. Two days— still nothing. "When is he going to poop? What are we doing wrong?" Finally on the third day, it happens! You weep with joy. You call your parents. "He pooped! We're going to be okay!"

Now you're headed down the daily "How was his poop?" path. From there, it's only a hop and a skip to Amazing Poop Stories. "That poop shot all the way across the room, hit the mirror, and ran down the wall. Look, you can still see the yellow stain, there, on the dancing bear wallpaper!" These stories are why your friends don't invite you to dinner anymore. (And you thought it was because they didn't like kids. Noooo. They don't like poop stories.)

When Dash was three and a half, he'd mastered peeing in the toilet, but pooping was another hurdle. For over a year, we had tried to get Dash to poop—not in his Batman underwear, not in the back yard—but in the potty. Every night we read him *Everybody Poops* (a hit with kids of all ages) and that classic, *Once Upon a Potty*. But nothing worked. Dash would still casually stroll behind the TV and look thoughtful. I'd screech, "Are you pooping?" And he'd turn to me, his face contorted and blazing red, and squeak, "No!"

It didn't help that both sets of grandparents would gasp, "He's still not toilet trained? We had you trained by the time you were thirteen months old." Yeah, sure. . . .

When Dash finally pooped in the potty, Malcolm and I went berserk with joy. We cheered, we gave presents, we put it in our holiday newsletter. And Dash was bursting with pride.

From then on, whenever Dash had to go, he'd announce at the top of his lungs, "Poop comin'!" This could clear a crowded aisle in seconds. Surly clerks would rush to unlock their "Employees Only" bathroom door and collapse in relief when Dash made it inside. But minutes later, the bathroom door would bang open and Dash would back his bare bottom into the store, demanding, "Somebody wipe me!"

You'd think once we passed the toilet training stage, we'd stop talking about poop. But it's getting worse. With the addition of our daughter, Skye, we now have an entire household scream-ing, "Does anyone have to poop?" "Mom! Come look at my poop!" "All right. There's poop on this towel—who did that?"

When I told my mother we were writing about poop, she couldn't believe it. "That's disgusting! How could you write such a thing?" A few minutes later she excused herself to take her Metamucil. I called after her, "You see, Mom? That's life. Poop happens."

Great Expectations

"**Y**eowwww!"

Each morning at 7:50 a.m. Malcolm bolts out of bed yelling, "School starts in thirty minutes. We overslept!"

This is my cue to race to the children's room and announce seriously, "Kids, we're late. I want you to get dressed this instant and get in the car."

Dash, being the oldest, gets the message right away and promptly starts looking under his bed for something to wear. On the other hand Skye seems paralyzed by this information and lies frozen, blinking her big blue eyes at me. Her limbs are like Jell-O. I snatch a pair of underwear from an open drawer and manage to get it on her. The clock is ticking. . .

Dash is already downstairs. I grab a dress from Skye's closet, and practically carry her to the kitchen, where Malcolm is slapping peanut butter and jelly on stale hot dog buns because we're out of bread. As Dash wolfs down his Toastie-Oaties, we realize that all his clothes are on inside out. A minute is lost debating whether he should undress and start over. We decide to let it go. It will be a new fashion statement. Skye refuses cereal and demands a Pop Tart. We're in luck—she likes them raw.

By this time Malcolm has finished the sandwiches. He stuffs them into the lunch boxes, and races out to start the car. Now begins the "Put on your shoes!" chant. It soon escalates from a gentle suggestion to a top-of-your-lungs threat: "If you don't put on your shoes and get in the car this instant, you'll be in time-out for the rest of your life!" Dash puts on his shoes.

Skye is still in her underwear, nibbling quietly on her Pop Tart and staring into space. She slowly turns to look at me and finally sees that my eyes are bulging and I am frothing at the mouth. It is 8:20. We are late.

Malcolm finishes Skye's Pop Tart and carries her, her dress, shoes, and coat to the car where Dash has already claimed the front seat. I race after them in my nightgown, clutching two glasses of water, two toothbrushes, and a hairbrush. We screech up to our school's drop off area—the "hug 'n go"— exactly ten minutes too late.

The kids race off. We sit in the school's driveway and take deep, calming breaths. I'm still in the backseat in my nightgown. Malcolm is staring numbly out the windshield. I notice that, just like Dash, he has bed-head and his shirt is inside out.

After nearly a minute of silence, Malcolm slowly turns to me and says, "Things have got to change."

I nod. "Tomorrow we have to get up earlier."

Malcolm's eye twitches. "How much earlier?"

We've been parents for eight years. If there's one thing we've learned it's not to set our sights too high.

"Five minutes," I reply. "And if that goes well, we'll try for ten."

"Agreed."

I raise one of the toothpaste glasses as a toast and, without thinking, down the entire thing.

Desperately Seeking Mary Poppins

Myrna (not her real name) just moved to Happydale (not a real town). She asked me to give her my baby sitter's phone number (not a good idea). I told her I would give her the name of other baby sitters, but mine was booked with me for the next five years. Now, some people might think that was mean-spirited. I don't care.

Myrna is a mom with four kids. She ought to know that the most sacred thing on the planet, besides your family photos, are your baby sitters' phone numbers. A good sitter can make or break your life.

There are some parents who will settle for any old sitter, as long as they are over six years old, can dial 911, and will accept two dollars an hour.

Not us. We learned our lesson the day our friend offered to have her "very responsible" fourteen-year-old son sit for us. He didn't seem like the caregiving type, but she absolutely, positively assured us that his two "extremely responsible" sisters, ages seven and nine, would be there to help. With great reluctance, we left Dash, who was three at the time, and Skye, just seven months old, with that crew.

When we returned several hours later, we found the son had gone fishing. The two little girls had let baby Skye roll off a very high bed onto a wood floor. Skye had an enormous lump and cut over her eye. She was crying so hard she'd broken out in hives. Dash was wandering around their backyard in a 20-pound diaper. He was alone and hadn't been changed or fed since we left.

We soon moved on to more "high school" types and mostly regretted it. My favorite moment was the night our seventeen-year-old sitter met us in the driveway. She was anxious to leave. We peeked inside the house and it looked like a massacre had happened.

The kids were sprawled on the kitchen floor and living room rug, face down. They were sound asleep. Dash and Skye were still in their clothes with filthy faces and hands. Empty baby bottles and toys were everywhere. And there was poop all over the rug. "That just happened," the sitter mumbled. "I meant to clean it up."

When we decided to opt for maturity the one grandmother we hired fell asleep on the couch in the middle of the afternoon. Our naked children were in the other room jumping on the furniture. The front door was wide open. A whole box of popsicles had been devoured. And there was granny, totally oblivious, snoring like a chain saw.

We finally discovered that you truly do get what you pay for. Now we only hire sitters who have majored in nursing and child psychology, and minored in physical education and art. Their hobbies are cooking and cleaning. They are stern disciplinarians, but are always lots of fun. They drive their own car and would never, ever consider having their tongues pierced. We have to pay them more than we earn. But hey, it's worth it!

In the Bleak Midwinter

This morning I spent an hour stuffing Skye and Dash into snow pants, parkas, boots, hoods, and mittens. They should be able to do that by themselves in five minutes. But it took an hour because we had to fight about every piece of clothing: "I hate turtlenecks." "Why do I have to wear long underwear?" "I can't get my boots on." "These pants are too uncomfortable." "Why do I have to wear this hood?" "I have to go to the bathroom."

I made the fatal mistake of putting my coat on first. By the time the children were dressed, I was dripping with sweat. Both kids were overheated from running away from me. I was frazzled from yelling at them. No way were we going to have a fun time playing in the snow. I wanted to bury them in it and dig them up sometime in the spring.

A few years ago, I had a morning not unlike today. Dash was two. Skye was a month old. We were living in Montana at the time. Our lake had frozen, and we decided to have a skating party. So our friends and Malcolm skipped down to the lake with the skates. I stayed behind to get the kids ready.

I put Skye in a snowsuit and stuffed her into a down baby bag. Dash, who was still in diapers, had to be changed, and then wrestled into each article of clothing. While I ran after him, Skye, who was boiling over inside her down bag, cried. By the time I got Dash dressed, I had to undress Skye to let her cool off. By then Dash was too hot and started to strip. Meanwhile, I could see Malcolm on the ice, skating merry circles with our friends. I shouted for him to come help, but he didn't hear me.

At this point, I should have punted. But I was mad. Mad at Malcolm for having fun. Mad at the kids for crying. Mad at the world for not telling me that two children would be so much harder than one. I was so mad that I slammed on a coat and gloves, shoved that screaming baby into her Snugli, and yanked Dash out of the house.

With the kids in tears, I marched down the steep snowy hill to the lake. At the spot where the log step was missing, I picked Dash up so he wouldn't fall. He didn't. But I sure did. Right onto a pointed rock. I actually broke my tailbone. It hurt so bad, I lay in the snow with the kids in my arms, and wept.

Did I go back to the house? Noooo. I limped to the ice, handed Malcolm the children and strapped on a pair of skates. I was going to have fun if it killed me. It nearly did.

I took two steps onto the ice and fell. This time I broke my leg in three places.

For the next eight weeks, I lay on my side with my leg in the air and Skye on my breast, wondering what happened to my life. Malcolm, who spent the next two months waiting on me, wondered what happened to his life.

The moral of this story? If you're going to have children, move to Florida until they're ten and can put on their own damn snow suits!

It's My Potty and I'll Poop If I Want To

The term "toilet training" is really a joke on parents. You don't train your children to use the toilet. You beg, threaten, and bribe them. And hope for the best.

Some kids are overachievers. I asked my friend Nadine when her daughter was toilet-trained. "One and a half," she replied. "It was a breeze. Katie just told us when she needed to go and we took her to the bathroom."

This was not the case with us. Dash was three and a half before he got his bodily functions under control. He was the only kid in his preschool who had to be changed by the teacher. We were certain he was going to be wearing Depends to his senior prom.

Susan and Jack's boy, Chase, wasn't toilet-trained until he was well past four. But Susan says she didn't sweat it. "The kids are ready when they're ready." And she's right.

The key to toilet training is to remember, it's not a horse race. Just because your neighbor's kid was out of diapers before he could walk, and all of your sister's children wore "big boy" and "big girl" underwear by the age of one, doesn't mean your child will do the same.

If you don't "go with the flow," everyone is going to wind up unhappy. You and your kid will feel like failures and the grandparents will second that emotion. They'll even offer great tips like, "Just put him on that potty chair and don't let him get up until he's done something important!"

Of course we didn't start out with the go-with-the-flow attitude. When Dash was one year old, we bought every style of potty chair available and placed them in the bathroom. But since Dash never went into the bathroom, we moved them to the kitchen. Finally, we had three potty chairs in the center of our living room.

They sat there for several years. Dash never actually peed in the potty chairs, but he did sit on them a whole lot. Who wouldn't? Every time he went near the things, we took pictures, gave him presents, and cheered.

A lot of parents make charts and hang them by the toilet. They give their kids stickers, stars, and M&Ms with each success. Sometimes it works. In our case it didn't. Basically, Dash never wanted to sit and pee. He liked standing.

We bought little tissue paper targets and floated them in the toilet. "Hit the bullseye, Dash!" He'd fire off a barrage of pee. Malcolm lit matches and hurled them into the toilet bowl. "Put out the fire, Dash!" Dash would aim his fire hose and douse the flames. He'd also hit the back of the toilet, the wall, and us. But who cared? Our little boy was peeing in the potty!

With Skye, we used an unusual tactic. One day I happened to find some pink and blue cake decorating sprinkles in the cupboard. On a whim, I asked Skye if she'd like to do a magic trick in the bathroom. "Yes, please, Mommy!"

I sprinkled the blue bottle into the toilet and said, "Pee on this blue magic dust and you can change its color to green." She leapt right onto the toilet seat. Sure enough, her yellow pee turned that blue to green. Later I grabbed the pink cake sprinkles. "Let's turn this pink to orange." This time Dash got into the act.

Soon every kid in the neighborhood wanted to pee in our potty. I finally just left the bottles on the back of the toilet and the kids and their friends used them whenever they wanted.

Larry and Coleen's daughter, Willa, wound up being toilet-trained on a long car trip. Knowing that the only reason Larry would pull over was if she had to throw up or pee, Willa started announcing she had to go to the bathroom. That allowed her to get out of the car and run around. For that, Willa had to go sit on a toilet in a public restroom and actually pee. And she did it.

Getting kids to pee in the potty is a big step. But getting them to poop in that same potty is a giant leap. Some people say children feel their poop is a vital part of them, like an arm or a leg. And the idea of just letting it go is agonizing. I believe that.

Linda and Dan's son Kenny was perfectly fine with peeing. But the instant he had to poop he'd demand a pull-up diaper.

Kenny just couldn't stand the feeling of something falling a great distance out of his bottom. It was scary.

Other kids won't let their bowels go until they know where their poop is headed. Our friend Tom arranged a tour of the local sewer plant for his son, Ben. Once Ben knew where his poop went, he was perfectly fine with using the toilet.

For our children, the leap to actually pooping in the toilet came by accident. When I caught Dash squatting outside in mid-poop, I scooped him up and ran to the bathroom. He finished pooping on the toilet. The same thing happened with Skye. Both of them realized that using the toilet wasn't so bad. (Of course, the dance of triumph and the gazillion presents Malcolm and I showered on them helped a little bit.)

At the start of every school year, thousands of parents of Huggie-clad toddlers panic about preschool. They're afraid they won't have time to get their kid out of diapers and into underwear before school starts.

Before you put your child in potty boot camp, check with your preschool about their rules. Skye's school preferred her to be totally trained, but they didn't mind dealing with some poop mistakes for a month or two, as long as they didn't have to wash out underwear. We kissed their feet and said, "Here's a supply of butt wipes, two dozen Winnie the Pooh panties, and if anything happens—throw Winnie and his poo in the trash." By the end of November, Skye was a skilled toileteer.

Malcolm and I had a little ceremony. We burned the diaper bag and gave the Huggies to our neighbor. After five years of one or both of our kids in diapers, we were finally free!

Don't Step on a Crack!

Baby's Progress Chart	
3 months	Baby rolls over
6 to 8 months	Baby sits up
10 to 14 months	Baby walks
14 months to 18 years	Baby jumps on your back!

Malcolm and I have an unspoken rule: Look both ways before you bend over. If you spot a young child within fifty feet of you, give them a stern look and this warning: "Don't even THINK about it." Once the warning has been given, keep your eyes glued to theirs, and quickly bend down and scoop up that lint, toy, or magazine lying on the floor. Never, I repeat, NEVER turn your back on your child.

I can't tell you how many times Malcolm and I have forgotten this rule, and lived to regret it.

I'll be shuffling across the living room with a cup of coffee in hand, minding my own business, when I'll notice a toy in the middle of the rug. Without a second thought, I'll bend over to pick it up. Suddenly, from out of nowhere—Dash leaps on my back. I scream, stumble forward, and bonk my head on the coffee table. My coffee splatters onto the rug and all over the couch.

You'd think my scream would be enough to scare my seventy-pound boy off my back. But nooooo . . . his arms are still wrapped around my neck, cutting off my air supply. He's giggling like a maniac, because I'm spinning in a circle, trying to swat at him with my empty coffee cup.

Once I finally get Dash off my back, I explain again, through clenched teeth, "Never, EVER jump on someone's back. You can really hurt them."

For some reason, this doesn't sink in.

My dad came to visit when Dash was three and Skye was one. He made the mistake of getting down on all fours. They were on him in a flash. The shock was so great, ol' Grandpa got whiplash. He was in a neck brace for the rest of the visit and for two months after that.

My friend Susan told me she was running a bath for her son Chase when she bent over to scoop a bar of soap from the bottom of the tub. Wham! He jumped on her back, and Susan went head first into the water.

It's become my single biggest excuse for not exercising. I'll put on a workout tape and stretch out on the carpet. Before I finish my first sit-up, both of the kids are on my back, and the dogs are licking my face.

We were at a soccer game on Saturday and our friend, Liandre, bent over to pick up her purse. Pow! She was ambushed from both sides by her twin five-year-olds. She staggered around for a few seconds, then fell spread-eagled on the grass. When I rushed to her aid, she looked up at me and said, wearily, "I suppose I'll miss it when they stop doing that, but for now it just wears me out."

Ain't it the truth.

Home Improvement, Family Style

Let's make a deal. We won't give your kid a "Let's Make an Authentic Weather Station!" if you don't give ours a "Let's Make a Panoramic Light Show!" On the surface, those kits seem great. "Fun for the whole family." But the whole family has nothing to do with it. The kids ripped open the "Let's Make a Sundial!" package I bought them last Christmas, found the paints, and immediately wanted to start painting. I explained that first they would have to glue every one of those little pieces of wood together, then draw tiny arcs and lines to number the hours and minutes before any painting could begin. They didn't want to do that. So I did it. For hours.

What began as a fun, family project had turned into a not-so-fun, Mommy-and-Daddy project. I asked myself: "Do I really need to be this creative?" I could be cleaning the garage. Or reading a book.

Malcolm and I shop at museum stores, anxious to give our children educational toys that will open their eyes to other cultures. But a Navajo pot kit just doesn't seem to work. While I'm carefully rolling out little worms of red clay and twisting them into a pot, my kid is making huge clay snakes and smashing them into the carpet. So I get mad and stuff my worms and paints back into the box, then shove the kit on the top shelf of the closet. Don't worry, it won't be lonely. It's up there with all of the other unfinished educational projects.

This past weekend, we discovered by total accident the greatest family project ever. Peeling wallpaper. Ever since we moved into our house two years ago, I've hated the shiny pink wallpaper in the hall. Finally I couldn't take it another minute. "I'm peeling this paper," I shouted. "Now!" The kids' eyes nearly popped out of their heads. "Can we help?" When I said yes, they grabbed big strips of the stuff and ripped them off the wall. You'd think they would grow bored. But Dash and Skye spent three whole days tearing that wallpaper. They were obsessed. We all were. We listened to old tapes, singing at the top of our lungs. We congratulated each other on a successful big peel. Cheered when the last piece came off. It was a blast.

From now on, we're just saying no to "Let's Put Something Together!" kits. We're only getting our kids things that they can take apart. We'll start small—clocks, toasters, VCRs. And with all of the money we've saved from not buying those "Let's Make a Useless Item!" kits, we're going to buy another house and let the kids destroy that!

Friends Before Children

Finally, Malcolm's old best friend, Ray, came for an overnight visit. Ray is a swell guy. But Ray falls into the category we call FBC—Friends Before Children.

FBCs are usually pals from the good old days when we were wild, crazy, and childless. Since they don't have kids, FBCs refuse to accept that we now have an eight-year-old son and a five-year-old daughter who occupy every waking hour of our lives.

They can't believe we haven't closed a bar in ten years. And they're shocked, absolutely shocked, to discover that we cut out school lunch menus from the newspaper, and have never missed a skate night.

These friends are vaguely aware that when Malcolm and I are alone, we do parent-type things. We worry about schools, drive Dash and Skye to soccer practice, and plan their yearly birthday parties. But FBCs don't want to hear about it.

FBCs want to talk about great art films. They read thick books with big words, and offer to lend them to us.

FBCs are up on all of the latest sitcoms. They have never heard of Rugrats, Elmo, Pokemon, or Legos.

They don't understand that we can't just jump in the car and go to dinner and a movie. They're certain there's an endless supply of baby sitters on 24-hour call.

When Malcolm and I get word that an FBC is about to drop in, we race to the video store and rent ten kids' movies. We order pizza for Dash and Skye to eat in front of the TV. We give the kids baths and put them in their pajamas somewhere around four in the afternoon.

Why? Because FBCs don't know how to integrate children into their universe. They think the baby announcements we sent out were for puppies. And that our "puppies" can be patted on the head, tossed a Milkbone, and locked in the basement while they are visiting.

FBCs are irritated that we can no longer give them our full attention. They're miffed that they can never finish a story or get to the punchline of a joke because we're having to wipe up spilled juice or referee a squabble.

But the worst thing about FBCs is they consider themselves authorities on parenting. On the third day of a visit, when Dash and Skye have begun to whine, fight, and beg for attention, an FBC will start clucking and tossing around words like "discipline," "boundaries," and "follow-through."

That's when Malcolm and I get up really early. We load the kids in the car, drive to a motel—and wait.

When we return we find a befuddled note that reads: "I got up and you guys were gone. I waited around as long as I could. I'm hungry. I guess I'll grab some lunch downtown and hit the road. It was great seeing you. Ciao! Uncle Ray. P.S. Give my love to Josh and Skylar."

Thanks for the Mammaries

My cousin Vikki always had enormous breasts, even before she breast-fed. But I'd never seen anything so shocking as the day I watched Vikki haul this huge casaba melon out of her bra and shove it into her daughter Kelsey's face. That was my first brush with breast-feeding.

When Vikki stopped breast-feeding, her doctor recommended she bind her breasts to help dry up her milk. He handed her an ace bandage. She took it home, put it on, then called the doctor. "I need another bandage." "How is that possible?" the doctor asked. Vikki explained that she had wrapped the bandage around one breast and tied it off at the end. "Now I need to wrap the other one."

The image of Vikki and her triple-F bra haunted me throughout my pregnancy. We were cousins. Our breasts were related. If I wasn't careful, I could end up sporting two bandaged torpedoes with bows at the tips. I thought, "Maybe if I consult an expert, this won't happen."

So I took a class in breast-feeding from Attila the Activist. Big mistake. The second Dash was born, there she was in my hospital room. She grabbed my breast, stuffed it into Dash's face, and barked at me, "Let down your milk!"

For the next two days she'd slink into my room and order me to breast-feed my baby. Finally I begged the nurses to bar her from the hospital. But that didn't stop Attila. Weeks later, she phoned me at home, and hissed, "Are we still using the breast?" Using the breast? To my friends and relatives, I had become the breast. They would beg to hold the baby, but the second Dash made a squeak, they'd point him at my chest. "I think he's hungry," they'd say. "Go back to Momma."

That's when I'd have a hormone surge and shriek, "Stay away from Momma. That baby couldn't possibly be hungry. I just fed him! All I do is feed him!"

My first public feedings were traumatic. While other mothers would subtly drape a small receiving blanket over one shoulder, I had to hide under a pup tent. And the tent had to cover my waist because that's where my breast landed when it kerthumped out of my nursing bra.

In those days, I would blush and sweat profusely while struggling to feed Dash without anyone seeing. But by the time I had Skye, I had become an exhibitionist. Not on purpose. I just quit worrying about offending people. I accepted that I was a mammal and that this was a natural act. People who were disgusted by the slurping sounds coming from under the pup tent would just have to get over it.

I stopped breast-feeding both kids at ten months. Mostly because I was tired of having milk squirt out of my chest whenever I heard a baby cry. It didn't even have to be my baby. I could be alone in a grocery store, some kid would wail—and the front of my shirt would be soaked. Once I had just been introduced to a young man, who made the mistake of saying, "Oh, you have a baby?" Milk shot out of both breasts like a water pistol. I looked up from my sopping chest and replied, "Take that as a warning. Never use the B word in front of me."

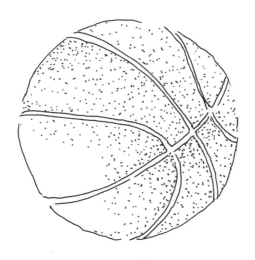

Slam, Dunk, and Roll

"Dad!" Dash shrieks. "We forgot to sign up for basketball!"

"Don't panic," Malcolm replies. "I'll get you on a team." He calls the YMCA and discovers the only way he can get Dash on a team is to be a coach. Gulp.

First Coaches Meeting

The bald guy on Malcolm's left raises his hand and says, "We should be allowed to run a full court press."

"What for?" demands the paunchy guy on his right.

"Because I'd like my kids to play some real basketball!" the bald guy answers.

"Are you a moron? These kids are in second grade!"

They lean across Malcolm, screaming insults at each other. The YMCA director blows his whistle. "Whoa, guys! Let's check the testosterone at the door!" Malcolm wonders if he can switch to coaching chess.

First Practice

Malcolm wants to start with a few drills. The kids want to shoot. Malcolm wants to teach them the basics. The kids want to shoot. Malcolm demonstrates a few moves. The kids want to shoot. Malcolm gives up. "Go ahead. Shoot."

First Game

Malcolm calls a huddle and lays out the game plan: "That's their hoop. This is our hoop. Put the ball in their hoop. Don't let them put it in our hoop."

The whistle blows. The children stand paralyzed. The parents go berserk, screaming, "Don't just stand there, do something! Be assertive! Steal the ball!"

Malcolm tries to ignore the parents and keep his cool. "Nick, inbound the ball!" Nick stares at him. "Like soccer," Malcolm explains. Nick's eyes light up. He tosses the ball overhead to Austin, who stops it with his chest, then dribbles it all the way down the court—with his feet.

During the second half, Molly bonks heads with Nick—they cry. Sam falls on the ball—he cries. The team can't dribble, run, or shoot. Malcolm cries.

Fifth Game

Malcolm's got a new game plan. Don't start Sam until his mom arrives. Otherwise he'll cry the entire time he's on the court. Give Julian a five minute warning that he's going in so he can run to the bathroom. Most important, hide the snacks until half-time.

Ten minutes into the game, Molly bursts into tears. She points at the boys. "No one will pass to me." Malcolm calls a time-out. "Please include Molly," he pleads with the others. "She's part of this team." During the next play, Dash flips Molly the ball, but she drops it. Dash gives his dad a "See?" look. Malcolm gives him a "Wait till we get home" glare.

Late in the second half, Dash gets tangled up with two defenders. Molly is wide open. "Pass the ball to Molly," Malcolm shouts. Dash shakes his head. "Pass the ball!" Finally, in desperation, Dash hurls the ball at her. Molly catches it, wheels, and—swish! Two points. Dash and Molly exchange high fives. The rest of the team cheers. Malcolm collapses on the bench, a complete wreck.

Frank

Before Malcolm and I had kids, we had Frank. Part Basset Hound, part Saint Bernard, he was half a dog high, and two dogs long. Frank was a person until our son Dash was born. Then he became a grumpy, stinky dog who hated children. It was a good thing Frank died before Dash was a year old. Otherwise, we would have had his teeth removed.

Now Frank has become The Greatest Dog Who Ever Lived memory for all of us, including Dash, who barely knew him, and Skye, who never met him. And even though Frank's dead and gone, he still plays an important role in our lives.

When the children are so full of big feelings that they don't know where to put them, they give them to Frank. The tears spill over and they wail, "I miss Frank!"

Two years ago I bought Dash's friend Henry a Robin Hood costume for his birthday. Dash saw the plumed hat and green cape and cried, "Can I have that?"

"No, it's for Henry."

"But Henry only likes guns and Star Trek-type toys," Dash told me.

"Really?" I said. Dash caught the look in my eye that said, "You're just saying that because you want the costume," and his chin started to quiver.

"Henry never, ever wears costumes, not even on Halloween," Dash cried in frustration. Sure, Dash wanted that Robin Hood costume, but he also knew Henry really would hate it. Finally the effort to reasonably explain was too much and Dash burst into tears. When I asked why he was crying, he blurted, "I'm thinking about Frank. Gosh, he was a great dog!"

Mourning Frank let Dash cry over a legitimately sad thing and not over the costume he couldn't have.

Sometimes our kids paint themselves into an emotional corner. They go ballistic—then don't know how to gracefully switch gears back to normal again. Frank is there to ease the way. Still wiping away tears, they'll ask, "Can Frank see me crying? Do you think he's in Doggy Heaven?" And we can move on without having to rehash the fight, or decide who was right or wrong.

My favorite Frank exchange went like this: Dash raced up to his sister with a measuring cup. "Skye, make yourself cry. I need some tears for my wizard's brew." Skye shut her eyes for a moment, then said, "I can't. You gotta hit me." "Think of something sad," Dash suggested. "Think of Frank."

Skye ran and stared at Frank's photo on the wall. Soon she said, "I feel the tears inside me. I feel them coming." Then Dash got an onion from the kitchen. "Here, sniff this. It'll help." He took a whiff and joined her beneath the picture. "Now I'm crying."

The two of them stood side by side, looking up at Frank and sobbing, while Dash caught their tears in his measuring cup. Sometimes I think we all could use a Frank for those times when the world is just a little too much, and our feelings a little too big.

If You Are What You Eat—
Then I Am a Compost Heap

Before I had kids, I ate what I wanted. Now I eat what the kids said they wanted, but don't want any more. Just this morning I sent the kids out to play, shuffled back to the breakfast table, and finished off Skye's bowl of soggy Captain Crunch. I can't stand Captain Crunch. And I used to hate soggy cereal.

Before I had kids, I didn't eat food that had fallen on a filthy carpet caked in dog hair. I would never have thought of finishing someone else's glass of milk, especially one with bits of food particles floating in it. And I would have rather died than eat the rest of a pre-gummed, totally mushy teething biscuit.

But since I had kids, I have done all those things. And I continue to do them on a daily basis. I think it has something to do with not wanting to waste food, but frankly some of those items no longer qualify as food.

In one of the zillion weight loss programs I have joined since I had children and gained 27 dress sizes, they recommended I keep a food journal. I was to write down everything I put in my mouth. I smugly thought, "Mine will be short and sweet, since I have stuck to my diet."

Here's a sample page from my diary, listing what I thought I ate, and what I actually ate:

Breakfast

Coffee, no cream; one slice dry toast, no butter

AND. . .

1 handful of Sugar Frosted Flakes, straight from the box

1 peanut butter-flavored crunch puff from Skye's bowl

the rest of Dash's orange juice and his Flintstone vitamin

4 rice cakes (from the bag I packed for Skye's lunchbox)

1 slice of ham and a handful of potato chips (intended for Dash's lunch)

Lunch

One diet Coke; one can Slim-Fast

AND. . .

Half a peanut butter sandwich (found by Skye's bed)

5 stale corn chips (lying on floor by TV)

3 Starburst candies (found in Dash's jeans)

A bowl of Orville Redenbacher popcorn (originally meant for kids' afternoon snack but they didn't touch it. Really.)

Dinner at Senor Sam's

Taco salad, no meat, no cheese, no sour cream, dressing on the side

AND...

the rest of Dash's burrito

3 of Skye's quesadillas

All of Skye's guacamole and sour cream

2 baskets of tortilla chips

no dessert

AND...

The rest of Skye's totally melted scoop of vanilla ice cream smothered in butterscotch syrup

2 half-eaten Peppermint Patties

After the shock of reading the above journal entry (my first and last one), I knew I needed to do some serious cutting back.

So I got rid of the bran toast, the diet Coke, and my case of Slim-Fast.

Put on Your Shoes

I read somewhere recently that the Top Five producers of stress are:

1. A death in the family
2. Terminal illness
3. Divorce
4. Money
5. Losing your job

Malcolm and I feel they left one out. The Big One. The one responsible for the twitch in my right eye, Malcolm's thinning hair, and the startling rise in our blood pressures: Getting children to put on their clothes!

Just writing that sentence makes the veins pop out in my neck. Every morning we engage in the "Put on Your Clothes!" battle with Skye. Some days are better than others. A few tears, and she's dressed. But really bad days involve running, tackling, screaming, drawer-emptying, and door-slamming. These acts are all committed by me because my blow-your-top meter no longer has a midrange. I just go from 1 to 100.

Skye's role in this war of wills consists of saying no, running away, and my favorite—stripping off the clothes you have just spent forty-five minutes getting her to put on.

She has a closet full of the cutest outfits imaginable, all chosen with care by both grandmas and Aunt Debbie, and mailed to her in beautifully wrapped packages. These outfits are not acceptable to our little princess because—"That dress has pockets," or, "That skirt won't twirl," or, "That top has pink flowers, I only like blue."

There was a time when I actually cut the pockets off several very pretty dresses. They all had this bizarre U-shaped outline of a seam on the front. I supposed I could have just sewn the pockets shut but that would have required a domestic skill I don't have. (I always say, if it can't be cut, staple-gunned, or duct-taped, it doesn't belong in our closets!)

Finally I wised up. I realized that no matter what we bought for Skye, it would be wrong. In fact, the more expensive the clothing item, the less chance it had of ever being worn. So I stopped buying Skye clothes altogether. Which is why, when we opened her closet this morning, she had nothing to wear.

So Skye went to school dressed in a swimsuit bottom (she's outgrown her underwear), polka dot leggings pulled from the dirty clothes, and a stained T-shirt with short sleeves. She wore two mismatched socks and a pair of snow boots. We have no idea where her shoes are.

My friend Pam told me she used to have the same problem with her son Austin. For five years she chased him around the house, trying to get him dressed. Then she wasted another hour looking for his shoes. But she came up with her own unique solution. Now, every night after supper, Pam and Austin pick out his outfit for the next day. They sing a song, read a book, and he goes to bed—fully clothed in his jeans, shirt, sweater, and shoes.

We'd try that with Skye, but she will only sleep naked.

Code Words

Fred is our friend. We like Fred and his family a lot. His son, Justin, is Dash's good friend. Fred is smart and funny, and generally good company. But Fred has a big flaw—his temper. On the temper meter, when the rest of us hit ten, Fred hits twenty. Steam blows out of his ears. His already big voice booms. And foul language fills the air.

Most people don't get the opportunity to see Fred blow his top. Only his close family friends. We fall into that category and, unfortunately, so do our kids.

We recently took a trip with Fred and his family. By about Day Four, Dash and Justin were getting on each other's nerves, and Skye was getting on EVERYONE's nerves. Put the three kids together in the back seat of a hot van, squeeze four big adults into the other seats, and you've got Fred primed and ready for a major explosion.

When Fred finally did erupt, it was all directed at Dash. The force of his anger and the terrible language Fred used really had a big effect on all of us. I'm sure Dash will remember that moment for the rest of his life.

I had a talk with Fred, and that evening I had a talk with the kids. I let them know that Fred was absolutely in the wrong. No matter how upset you get at someone, there is never any reason to use that kind of language. We talked about Fred's problem with handling his anger. My children mentioned kids they knew at school who had the same problem. "Those kids usually hit people," Dash said. "Fred was hitting with words," Skye added.

Then we discussed the incident that led to Fred's explosion. Fred had listened to me ask Dash to stop doing something at least five times. I was frustrated, and Fred was frustrated hearing me be ignored. I told the kids that I didn't like yelling at them over and over. I felt like I was just spewing endless sentences that they didn't hear. So I asked Dash and Skye if we could come up with one word that would let them know that whatever they were doing had to stop that instant. It would be our secret code word. They looked at each other and grinned. "Fred."

It's been three months since the infamous Krakatoa Temper tantrum, and our secret code is still working like a charm. Whenever the kids get themselves wound into a knot of whining and picking on each other, I just have to say the magic word—and they stop. In fact, it's so effective that people give us funny looks, wondering what just happened. Even Fred.

The kids just smile. It's our little secret.

Happy Birthday, Baby!

Dash's birthday was this week. Our boy has now been around the sun eight times. It's hard to believe he's made it this far with such incompetent parents.

Before Dash was born, Malcolm and I took breathing and breast-feeding classes. We watched horrifying films about natural childbirth. (Can you tell I opted for drugs?) My bible was *What to Expect When You're Expecting*, a week-by-week description of what's growing inside you.

For nine months our entire focus was on Opening Night. We forgot to think about the Long Run. Or even Day Two. So when the nurse handed us our little bundle of joy, Malcolm and I looked at each other and cried, "We're not ready!"

We hit the panic button. "What if we drop the baby? Or accidentally smother him? Or poison him? Or forget we have him and leave him in the car?"

Although it was a warm spring day when we left the hospital, Dash looked like Nanook of the North, swaddled in sleeper, sweater, down-filled baby bag and knit cap. A friend said, "He looks a little redfaced, maybe you should loosen his clothes." "Are you kidding?" we cried. "What if the wind blows? He could catch pneumonia!" For his first diaper change we seatbelted Dash onto the changing table and surrounded it with pillows (just in case the belt broke and Dash hurled himself to the floor). Then we went through eight diapers before finally figuring out how to get the Vaseline on his belly button and not on the sticky diaper tabs.

That evening I dropped a dishpan and Dash didn't react. I turned to Malcolm in a panic. "Do you think our baby is deaf?" Malcolm ran several tests which included hand claps and door slams. Dash flinched at every sound. But he didn't blink. Malcolm turned to me and said solemnly, "He's not deaf, but he could be blind."

By Day Three, Dash wasn't sleeping through the night. How could he? I was so afraid he might suffocate that I woke him up every half hour to make sure he was alive.

"We can't put it off any longer," Malcolm declared on Day Five. "We have to give him a bath." I panicked. "I don't know how!" Malcolm suggested we just hold him under the faucet. "Are you kidding? The nurse gave us specific instructions. We just have to find that piece of paper." When I did, we lined up in front of the sink with every form of bathing equipment that's been invented. Then I slowly read, "A. Wash head. B. Wash body."

At the end of the first week, Malcolm and I were talking while we changed Dash's diaper. Still talking, we left the room. It wasn't until we were out the front door that we realized, "We left the baby on the changing table!" We nearly killed each other trying to get through the door at the same time.

We're now at Day 2,925. This morning Dash fixed himself breakfast, packed his lunch, and, although it was a warm spring day, allowed us to smother him in a down parka, mittens, and knit cap. You see, no matter how old he gets, he will still be our little baby boy.

The Art of Living

Kirsten and John are remarkable people. They each wear many hats—parent, actor, potter, woodworker, gardener. But their real occupation is artist. They are truly artists at living.

Kirsten and John have a beautiful six-year-old daughter, Isabella, and a house and the most magnificent garden in our town. John throws clay pots and Kirsten sews beautiful clothes. They have modest incomes, yet always look stylish. They work full-time jobs with crazy schedules, yet they always manage to find time to volunteer for charities and at school.

At potlucks, Malcolm and I bring beans and weenies in Tupperware containers with our names masking-taped to the plastic lid. Kirsten and John bring fresh baked bread in a willow basket and pasta and fresh pesto from their garden served up in a blue glazed bowl.

No matter what the function, Kirsten always brings a little gift for the host or hostess—usually a beautifully labeled jar of homemade jam or two beeswax candles tied with a pretty ribbon.

Birthday presents are usually wrapped in paper decorated by Isabella and her parents, tied with a pretty grosgrain ribbon. And their cards are always exquisitely handmade.

On the first day of school this year, Isabella presented her teacher with a big bouquet of sunflowers picked from her garden.

When our children play with Isabella they do fun things like bake apple strudel with Kirsten or throw cock-eyed birdbaths on John's potter's wheel.

The highlight of every fall is Kirsten and John's Stone Soup party. Kirsten reads the famous story to all of the children at the party, then each child is assigned a role from the story. They dress in costume and set about making stone soup.

The Mayor harvests the corn. The Banker and her husband pick the tomatoes. The Bakers gather green beans and the Soldiers dig for potatoes and onions. The Butcher pulls the carrots and the Town Dog picks the squash.

The adults wash and chop the vegetables. Then the children drop a stone and their vegetables into a big cast iron pot that has been simmering on the open fire by Kirsten and John's gazebo.

After the soup is done, we families sit in a big circle on the lawn and slurp spoonfuls of soup while munching great hunks of homemade bread.

When things get out of hand here at Camp Run-a-Muck-a, Malcolm and I always look to Kirsten and John for inspiration. They don't have any more hours in the day than we do. Yet somehow they manage to take such care with the time they have. They treat the daily events of their lives as celebrations and simple gifts as works of art.

When we grow up, we want to be Kirsten and John.

M Is for Me

Last Sunday was my monthly women's dinner. As usual, I was running late, and hadn't put on any make-up when my ride pulled into the driveway. Now, make-up is an absolute requirement at a women's dinner because your women friends are the only ones who care about what you look like. So I grabbed the coat with the biggest pockets, hoping it might hold a hidden lipstick or mascara.

Once in the car, I dug in my pocket and pulled out a pair of Skye's underwear, Dash's mitten, and a half-eaten sandwich. My friend looked at me and said, "There's no question who the mom is in this car." Boy, was she right. It wasn't just the contents of my pocket that marked me as a parent. It was everything about me. My friend looked like a sleek, stylish woman of the new millennium. I looked like a deranged den mother.

I was mortified. When I got home I threw open my closet doors and wailed, "Where is it written that once you have children you have to wear drop-waist jumpers with huge pockets and blouses with Peter Pan collars? Nowhere. So why do I have an entire closet full of this stuff?"

Malcolm, who was already asleep, muttered, "What are you talking about?"

"I used to have some sense of style," I blubbered. "I used to put on mascara, and comb my hair, and wear all black. Now I can't find my make-up, I don't have time to brush my hair, and none of my black clothes fit."

He struggled to open his eyes. "Did something happen at your dinner?"

"My jumpers are covered in silly daisies and Mary Engelbreit watering cans. I wear sensible flats. I even have the regulation Mom's haircut—short and forgettable."

"So?"

"I blend in with every other mother. Strange kids hand me their half-eaten ice cream cones. They wipe their noses on my skirt. And what's worse, if they have a runny nose and I don't have a Kleenex, I'll wipe their nose on my skirt."

"You do that?" Now Malcolm was awake.

I slumped on the bed. "I'm not a person anymore. I'm a mom."

"What's wrong with being a mom?"

"Nothing. I just don't want to be *only* that. I'm tired of being perky. I want to look sleek, mysterious—"

"Then why don't you just buy some new clothes?" He yawned.

That was it. The key to my transformation back into a woman of the world was a new wardrobe. We agreed that I should go shopping.

I bought a form-fitting top, stylish short jacket and velvet pants—all in black. I put them on. For fifteen minutes, I was sleek, I was mysterious. Then Skye wiped her mouth on my blouse, I fell back on the couch and my jacket was instantly covered in dog hair. The good news is—I found my mascara. It had been wedged between the couch cushions and was now stuck to the bottom of my new velvet pants.

The Joy of Cooking

Whenever things get a little too quiet around our house, Malcolm and I get worried. It usually means Dash and Skye are up to something. This can run the spectrum from carving their initials in the furniture to giving each other haircuts. And lately, cooking. Most people think cooking sounds like a nice, instructive family activity. But in our house, instructions have nothing to do with it.

Cooking means two kids throw a lot of mysterious ingredients into a bowl and two adults have to eat it. The following are some recipes you will never find in *Good Housekeeping*. They were crafted in our test kitchen by our own little galloping gourmets.

Dash and Skye's Recipe for Ten Pound Cake

All of the eggs in the refrigerator (shells optional)

A bag of flour

3 handfuls of sugar

What's left in the milk carton

That box of baking soda in the back of the fridge (not to be confused with baking powder)

1 bag corn nuts

Mix and pour ingredients into casserole dish. Put in oven. Tell Mom and Dad you're baking a cake. When Dad rushes in, panicked that you're burning the house down, ask him to turn on the oven. After the cake is done, cover with two inches of blue frosting. Make sure to get blue food coloring all over the counters, floors, and on your clothes. (For extra bonus points, lose lid to food coloring bottle.)

Decorate cake with two bags of red hots. Take Mom a huge slice. Watch her to make sure she eats the whole thing. If she says, "Mmmm! This is just the way I like it—hard on the outside and spongy on the inside, with powdery pockets of baking soda and crunchy corn nuts," make her eat another piece. Twice as big.

For a near death experience, why not try:

Skye's To-Die-For Shake

Half a can of chocolate syrup

What's left of Mrs. Butterworth's maple syrup

Some ice cream

Half a bottle of calamine lotion (The secret ingredient!)

Mix everything together in a tall glass. Give it to your best friend, Katie. After she throws up pink barf, tell Mom and Dad that Katie is sick. When they call the Poison Control hotline, swear Katie didn't drink any calamine lotion and if she did it was, "maybe just a little bit, but you see, we needed some pink to go with the brown and white."

After Dad and Mom have called two pediatricians, one homeopath, and a pharmacist to be told that Katie will live, and after Katie's mom has driven ninety miles an hour to get from her job in the next town to your house, do not ask if Katie can come over tomorrow.

Katie's mom will then let your mom know exactly what she thinks of her baby-sitting skills. And even six months later, when you think the whole event is forgotten and Katie comes back for a visit, she will announce, "I am not allowed to eat or drink anything in this house. I have brought my own food and water."

Cleanliness Is Next to Impossible

When Dash was born, my mom had a small cold. I insisted she wear a surgical mask before she came within ten feet of him.

Malcolm and I were hysterical about crowds—too many people with too many germs. Every time we'd go out, little snot-nosed kids would want to hug and kiss the baby. I'd nearly have a heart attack.

For the first year, Malcolm and I sterilized everything. We ran nipples and bottles through the dishwasher and then, just to be on the safe side, we boiled them on the stove.

If Dash didn't finish his formula, instead of putting the nearly full bottle back in the fridge, we'd throw it away. It was contaminated!

If a teething biscuit or cracker even touched the kitchen floor, we'd toss the filthy thing in the garbage disposal. We even talked about shaving the dogs to cut down on dog hair.

At first we worried that everything we did would kill him. Then we realized that almost nothing could. Little by little, we started to relax.

This happens to every parent. Just ask anyone who has ever given their child a pacifier how they cleaned it in the first month, and how they cleaned it in the second year. Their answer will go something like this:

Age 1 to 6 months

Sterilize pacifier on stove for ten minutes in boiling water. Dry with clean white cloth.

6 to 8 months

Microwave cup of water for one minute, dip pacifier in cup. Dry with dish towel.

8 to 10 months

Run under hot water faucet, don't bother to dry.

10 to 12 months

Run under cold water. Wipe on shirt.

1 to 3 years

Lick it and shove it back in your kid's mouth.

Now, five years later, I have to confess that there have been times when I have served the kids cereal for breakfast in bowls that I'm not quite sure have been washed or just licked clean by the dogs. But hey! What they don't know won't hurt them.

The Pits Stop

For years I couldn't get on an airplane because I was deathly afraid of flying. Then Malcolm and I took a 2,500 mile car trip with Dash, who was then two years old, and I was cured. We thought we were going to tour the natural wonders of the west—Monument Valley, the Grand Canyon, and Yosemite. But Dash had a different plan. He wanted to go to McDonald's.

Somewhere between Montana and Colorado, Dash spotted the golden arches and screeched his very first sentence: "I see one, Daddy!" From then on, he never let up. We had to stop at every single McDonald's along the way.

Why? Because of the Playlands. Kids love 'em. They have ball pits, climbing tubes, and are completely enclosed by a rope cage that keeps grown-ups out. The only way in is through a tiny tube barely big enough for a six-year-old.

During our trip I'd sit on a bench with the other moms, clutching my Diet Coke, and watch Dash climb up the slide and hurl himself into the plastic balls. About every three minutes I'd shout, "Watch what you're doing. You just jumped on that little girl!" Dash didn't listen, but it let the other benchwarmers know I cared.

After fifteen minutes, it would be time to leave. The Mom Brigade would approach the yellow plastic tube. "Come on," we'd shout, "it's time to go." Dash, who was safely tucked away behind the ropes, would look me straight in the eye and say, "No!" I'd ask nicely. No again. I'd plead, explaining that we had a very long car ride ahead. Still no. Finally, I'd reach through the ropes and grab at his shirt. He'd skitter away, disappearing back into the tubes with the other rotten kids.

We mothers would take turns shoving our twisted, red faces up that tube and bellowing, "I'm counting to ten and then I'm leaving. I mean it! And when you get out of there, boy, are you going to get it!"

The sweat would pour down my face because I knew one of us was going to have to "go in." And as the unlucky volunteer squeezed herself into the tiny yellow tube, we'd shout helpful words of advice like, "Stay away from the ball pit. I lost my shoes in there. The bottom's full of moldy McNuggets!"

Finally, the kids would realize we meant business. One by one they'd careen down the slide, slamming into the mom wedged halfway up the tube. I'd extract Dash from the tangle of bodies and drag him through the parking lot to our van. By the time he was belted into his car seat, I was a mass of quivering Jell-O.

So after an adventure like that, how could we possibly think it a good idea to put a five-year-old and a seven-year-old in a van and drive 1500 miles to Disneyland? The answer is clear—we were insane!

What I Learned on Our Trip to Disneyland

---

1. The minute you pull out of the driveway, your daughter will start asking, "Are we there yet?" This will continue for the next eight hours.

2. If you pack a lunch to eat in the car, it will be devoured before you reach the freeway entrance.

3. There are only so many times a person can listen to Goofy singing, "There's a hole in my bucket."

4. When you take your daughter to pee at the last rest stop for a hundred and twelve miles, it's guaranteed that she will have to poop as soon as you're back on the freeway.

5. McDonald's will always be out of the Happy Meal toy that your son wants. And he will blame you.

6. If you are trying to separate your screaming kids while driving, you will swerve across two lanes of traffic and nearly hit the overpass.

7. If you spend the entire car ride telling your kids about the fun they're going to have on The Pirates of the Caribbean, it will be closed for repairs.

8. If you pay $50 for autograph books signed by all the Disney characters, they will lie forgotten under the car seat next to the Mickey Mouse ears your kids just had to have or they'd die!

9. If you sit in the first thirteen rows of any show at Sea World—you will get soaked. And you will be cold. And you will march directly to the nearest tee-shirt shop and pay a hundred dollars for four ugly sweatshirts, just so you can be warm and dry.

10. When you finally pull into your own driveway it will be ten o'clock at night and your kids will be asleep. As you drag your weary body out of the car and carry your sleeping angels up to their own beds, you will realize there really is, "no place like home."

Battle Scars

My friend Alice announced she was pregnant and I raced out to buy her the pregnant gal's bible: *What to Expect When You're Expecting*. I gave it to her at a family picnic.

Terry, one of the moms at our gathering, flipped through the book and asked, "Where's the chapter on battle scars?"

"What do you mean?" Alice asked, with alarm in her eyes.

"I lost a tooth when I gave birth to Shannon." Terry showed the group her fake incisor. "They were all loose while I was pregnant, but this is the one that fell out."

That prompted me to show my bald spot. It's on the right side of my head. "When you're pregnant your hair gets really thick and luxurious," I explained to Alice. "But after you have the baby, it all falls out." Alice gasped and I quickly reassured her, "Most of it comes back. But after I had Skye, this one little spot just wouldn't grow back."

Sally, who has the straightest hair on the planet, said her hair used to be curly until she had Blake. Denise, whose hair is a big mass of frizzy curls, had straight hair until five years ago when Eli was born. Katie turned temporarily gray at her roots when she was in labor with Annie.

Julia always had 20/20 vision. Then one morning, during her seventh month of pregnancy, she woke up and couldn't see a thing. Now she wears thick glasses. The same thing happened to Denise, only she wears contacts.

Cindy developed varicose veins during her pregnancy. So did Terry. And all of us, without exception, gained a shoe size.

Alice was in shock. "I'd heard you could get stretch marks but. . . ."

Alice never got to finish her sentence. The group of mothers went berserk, showing each other their little silver scars. Most of us have them on our stomachs. But some of the women, the thin ones, have stretch marks on their sides and back. And everyone has silver streaks somewhere on their breasts.

"And speaking of breasts," Cindy said, "I used to be a 36 B and now I'm a 38 Long." That prompted a group groan.

We all used to wear little lacy "barely there" bras. Now we wear steel reinforced things that lift, separate, and collapse exhausted in our dresser drawers at the end of the day.

Then I remembered my growths. The kids call them my Dash and Skye bumps. Dash's is on my knee and Skye's is on my breasts. Both are moles that grew while I was pregnant with the kids. I showed the gathering my bumps. I had to. They'd shown me their stretch marks.

We were about to tell Alice that, despite these horrible war stories, having a baby was worth every lump, bump, scar, vein, and lost tooth. But Alice, who was looking a little green around the gills, suddenly leapt up and ran from our circle with her hands clapped over mouth. We moms looked at each other and smiled knowingly.

"Morning sickness. That's one we left out."

Out of the Mouths of Babes

Yesterday I was doing chauffeur duty, taking Dash to soccer, and Skye and her best friend, Katie, to ballet class. The girls were in the back seat playing their favorite game, "What if?"

"What if I was a unicorn and you were my mommy, and the Abdominal Snowman was after us?" Skye said to Katie. "The Abdominal Snowman!" Katie gasped. "He's really scary." "They must have meant the Abdominal Crunches," Malcolm said later. "Now those are scary!"

That got me thinking about some of the other cute things our kids have said. I still remember the day Dash told me that, "Women are blootiful. But me and Dad are 'stinguished."

One of Malcolm's favorite moments was when Dash pulled him over to the cage in the corner of his classroom to show him the "skinny pigs."

I've been keeping a journal over the past few years, jotting down the funny, sweet, strange things the kids have said. I thought I'd share a few of them with you.

One day Dash was counting pennies. I held up the side with Lincoln on it and asked, "Do you know this man's name?" Dash stared hard at the coin and finally said, "Um . . . Derek?"

Valentine's Day, and three-year-old Skye announced, "I'm in wub with Ben. When I grow up to be a princess and Ben is a prince, I will dance with him in my gown of roses."

Dash, after taking a chairlift to the top of Big Mountain, flung his arms open and shouted, "Look, everybody! It's the whole wide world!"

Two-year-old Skye describing her bald grandfather: "Grampa has off hair. Grandma pulled it off."

Once Malcolm asked Dash why he was so mad at Skye: "She always hits me back!"

When Skye had the flu and threw up, she declared, "A mean guy came and put barf in me."

After a hard day at preschool Dash confessed, "I don't like Margaret's kisses. Margaret's kisses aren't real. They fall off."

Skye was helping me get dressed one morning. "Mommy, here's your skirt," she said. "And you can wear this top. Or you can just wear your breasts."

I think my favorite thing Dash ever said was when Malcolm had to go away on a business trip. On the fifth day Dash came to me and said, "Momma, my eyes hurt from watching for Daddy."

I'm sure all of you have favorite quotes from your kids. Art Linkletter was right—kids do say the darndest things!

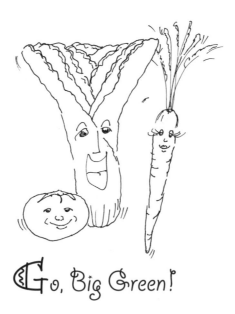

Go, Big Green!

When Dash's preschool had the nerve to serve him salad for lunch he stood up and yelled, "Where's the garbage? We don't eat this stuff at our house!"

Malcolm told his teacher that, of course, we ate salad, but we hadn't introduced it to Dash yet. We thought the proper food order was formula, rice cereal, baby food, Twinkies, hot dogs, Pop-Tarts, pizza, and then vegetables.

Dash and Skye spent their formative years snacking on soggy teething biscuits, turkey sticks, and dry Cheerios. I did see the odd kid gumming a broccoli spear but never assumed that was the norm.

Now that we've moved to Oregon, the land of Birkenstocks and blue-green algae, we've learned differently. People here say "tofu dog" and mean it. About a month after we settled in our healthy town, Dash invited a friend over to play. When I offered him popcorn as a snack, the kid asked, "Do you have any brewer's yeast?" I blinked several times and replied, "Do people really eat that stuff?"

Since he began second grade, Dash has tried, on his own, to eat lettuce. He'll take a bite, gag, and choke it down. I tell him, "Don't eat it if it makes you gag. You can't force yourself to like something."

Malcolm and I both remember gagging down green beans in elementary school. You know, the ones soaked in formaldehyde and served up in school cafeterias? You weren't allowed to go to recess until you had cleaned your entire plate. I would get a mouthful of beans, take a pretend drink of milk, and spit them into my milk carton.

Occasionally my parents would do the "sit there until you're finished" routine, which meant my brother and I would sit stubbornly at the table until eleven o'clock at night, staring at a plate of purple beets and big, ugly lima beans.

These days Dash asks for lettuce and tomatoes on his hamburgers and sandwiches. But five-year-old Skye will go to someone's house for dinner, look at her plate, and announce indignantly, "I can't eat this, it has vegetables in it!" Being the polite child she is, Skye will add, "Somebody bring me a peanut butter and honey sandwich!" She will then pause for a fraction of a second, and shout, "I said, I need a peanut butter sandwich!" But that's another issue. . . .

Last night we had a major breakthrough. The kids ate zucchini, green beans, tomatoes, and onions. Okay, the vegetables were cleverly disguised in spaghetti sauce and had been sliced and diced beyond recognition. But the kids knew what they were eating. And liked it. Score one for the Jolly Green Giant.

Cry Baby

There are few sounds more grating to my nerves than fingernails squealing across a chalkboard. The loud squeak that rubber boots make on snow is one of them. The high-pitched whine of Skye's voice when she's tired and upset is another. And the baby who cried behind me on yesterday's flight now tops the list.

I'm usually pretty understanding about crying babies on planes. I always worry about their ears. But this kid started bawling well before take-off. Her screaming began the instant she was strapped into her car seat. It continued, almost non-stop, for the next six hours. Her voice was so shrill that many passengers rode with their hands covering their ears.

If she was my baby, I would have had a nervous breakdown. But this baby's mother was cool as a cucumber. While her screaming kid struggled in vain to get out of her car seat, this woman casually flipped through a magazine. She was totally oblivious to the fact that her child was shredding the nerves of every passenger on that plane.

As I listened to that baby reach pitches that only a dog could hear, I remembered the lengths Malcolm and I went to trying to get our kids to stop crying.

After the first round of diaper-changing, bottle-feeding, ear-checking, temperature-taking, and gum-numbing, we would strip them naked. I don't know if it was the embarrassment factor or feeling breezes where the wind didn't usually blow that made our kids pause—but it was usually good for a few minutes of silence.

And after a long crying jag, just a few minutes of quiet was a lifesaver. And that's when we invented the surprise attack. Suddenly popping up in a weird hat or singing a very loud note would make our children pause long enough so we could take a couple of Advil.

I found an abrupt change of temperature, like sticking the kid's head in the freezer or stepping outside in a blizzard also was good for a startled, "Huh?" Malcolm discovered that suddenly turning our stereo up to 10 could shock our kid (and every other kid in the neighborhood) into stunned silence.

Of course, some of those things you can't do on a plane. But if she was my baby, I would have spent that six hour flight giving dramatic readings of *Baby in the Box* and *Find the Duck*, leading "Twinkle, Twinkle, Little Star" sing-alongs, and apologizing profusely to anyone who would look me in the eye. I would have handed my baby toys, rattles, puppets, and food. I would have tickled, hugged, and bounced my baby until my arms ached.

And at the end of the flight I would have been dripping with sweat, covered in hives, and exhausted from giving my baby the greatest performance of my life.

But that wasn't my baby—and boy, am I glad!

Pet Cemetery

In choosing a pet, you need to ask yourself one question: In the end, will this be a shoebox funeral or a toilet funeral?

Gerbils, guinea pigs, rats, snakes, and ferrets qualify for a Buster Brown service. Goldfish, lizards, frogs, and mice fall into the "burial at sea" category.

The first time your kid comes to you and asks, "Can I have a puppy?" you make a choice. You either go with the puppy, like our friend Donna did, or you find other pet options.

Donna has three children under the age of six. Garth, the baby, was only five months old when daddy Bill brought home Oggie Doggie.

It's now one year later. Donna and Bill are divorced. The kids divide their time between their parents' apartments. And Oggie, the immense golden Lab, lives by himself in the ruins of their house. He sleeps on their shredded chintz couch and pads up and down the once-carpeted stairs (the back yard is strewn with hunks of chewed carpet). Their Stickley table with the gnawed legs was sold at a garage sale. And their baby sitter, who tried to watch three toddlers AND a dog with feet bigger than her own, has dropped her lawsuit (her shoulder was dislocated when she tried to take the beast for a walk).

We already had two grown dogs when our kids came to us begging for a puppy. Remembering our poor friends, Donna and Bill, we were firm. No puppy. No kitty. Maybe a lizard.

The pet store owner told us to put Danger (the lizard) in a glass tank. "Just look at him," he told the kids. "Don't hold him." Since a lizard only eats live crickets, the owner suggested we buy a big bag of crickets to feed Danger. We could store the crickets in a jar. Every three days we were to feed Danger a sacrificial meal.

When we got home and were busily punching holes in a jar lid, I thought, "Why keep the crickets in this jar? Why not just put them in the tank with the lizard? When Danger gets hungry, he can just grab a snack. All we have to do is give him water."

Well. . . . Ten days later, we noticed several crickets the size of grasshoppers thumping around inside the tank. Danger was nowhere to be found.

No one told us that lizards only eat when they're hungry, or that crickets eat whenever they feel like it. Which is all the time.

When we lifted the plastic log, we found ol' Danger, dead as a doornail. He'd been murdered by his dinner!

We gave Danger the royal flush. Just like Swimmer and Float, our deceased goldfish. And Yertle the poor squashed turtle.

We finally stopped our Tidy Bowl farewells the day our neighbor, Mrs. Kranzler, passed away. The kids were totally distraught. Not about her death. But about her size. "There is no way Mrs. Kranzler will ever fit down that toilet!"

Funny Valentines

This week I wheeled my cart into the check-out line at Safeway and froze. A big-breasted woman in hot-pink spandex stared at me from the cover of a magazine. Underneath her picture was this life-shattering question: "Is the Thrill Gone? Ten Tips to Put Romance Back Into Your Marriage."

I reached for the magazine and flipped to the article. It included a test you take to be sure the thrill is gone. "Of course it's gone," I muttered. "We have two kids." I skipped to the tips:

1. Pamper yourself. Buy a pair of lacy, silk underwear.
2. Tonight, when your husband comes home from work, surprise him with a candlelight dinner.

I couldn't even get to tip number three. First of all, me in a pair of big girl lace panties is no more attractive than me in a pair of big girl cotton pants. And no way can we have candles in our house. Every time I light one, some kid sings "Happy Birthday" and blows it out.

I stuffed the magazine back in the rack in disgust, paid for my groceries, and stomped out of Safeway. But on the way home I started to worry.

Maybe the thrill was gone. When Malcolm and I were dating, one of us would drive twelve hours to visit the other every weekend. We'd write endless letters quoting Yeats and Edna St. Vincent Millay. I'd weep if I missed Malcolm's call. But that was courtship. Who could keep up that passionate frenzy?

We have friends who insist on arranging a date with each other once a week, sans kids. I don't know if it improves their love life, but at least they get to finish a sentence. Or a joke.

Other people we know leave town for romantic getaways. Some act like they're leaving town and check into a local motel. That cuts down on the "What if something happens and we can't get there in time?" worry.

The most romantic thing Malcolm and I have done lately is take ballroom dancing lessons. Once a week, we dance the fox-trot to wonderful old songs like "All of Me." It was great until one week when Malcolm reversed directions and I kept going forward. I nearly broke my nose on his chest.

When I got home from Safeway, I found Malcolm on the couch, with Skye and Dash nestled under each arm. He had been reading them *The Velveteen Rabbit*, and the kids had fallen asleep. So had Malcolm. His head was thrown back and wall-rattling snorts were coming from his open mouth.

At that moment, I realized the romance wasn't gone from our lives. It was just wearing a different face. A Velveteen Rabbit, very much loved, comfy-couch kind of face.

I wanted to hug and kiss each one of those sleeping angels. But then it hit me—My family was asleep. I had time to myself. I could watch a video, read a book. Or even take a bubble bath. Now that's what I call romantic!

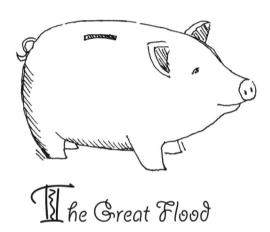

The Great Flood

DAY 1: A day that shall remain forever etched on our memories. Flood waters rampage through the heart of our little town in Oregon. The historic buildings circling the plaza are blasted with mud and water. Sixty-foot trees are stacked up like toothpicks in the park. The pavement on Main Street collapses from the weight of so much water. It's an amazing sight. Our home is only two blocks away but up a hill. So we escape the damage. But many friends aren't so lucky. Sixty-six houses are destroyed. The governor declares our town a disaster area. The good news: No lives are lost.

DAY 2: School is canceled. Sewer and water lines are broken. There is no running water. We tell Dash he can't take a shower until further notice. "Cool," he says. Friends call to report there are water trucks parked at the armory and elementary schools. A local grocery store has donated plastic jugs. But where do we go to the bathroom?

DAY 3: Still no water. Our neighbor calls. They've dug a hole in their back yard and filled it with lime. We're welcome to use it anytime. Oh, goody.

DAY 4: Dash and Skye see their destroyed park and playground for the first time and weep. They empty their piggy banks into a large glass jar. "We're going to fix the park."

DAY 5: Discover Dash and Skye have been using the upstairs toilet. Close lid and tape it shut. I can't wait to open it when the water comes back on.

DAY 6: Skye has the flu. We try to get her to throw up in backyard.

DAY 7: Portable toilets, trucked in by the National Guard, line the Safeway parking lot. Still no school. Skye's ballet and music classes are canceled. Dash's basketball practice is canceled. Malcolm is relieved. (He gets one more week to study the coaching manual.)

DAY 8: Temperatures drop. The Port-a-Potties are freezing and they are out of toilet paper. Our armpits are ripe and our hair is greasy. We're out of socks and underwear. I meet a class parent when I'm shopping for underwear. She has a well and septic tank, but no road. Dash invites her and her four children to move in with us. She says thanks but declines. (Phew!)

DAY 9: Big news! The Holiday Inn (20 miles away) is renting rooms with showers for $30 a night. We call for reservations. They're full. I burst into tears. Skye tries to console me, offering a box of baby butt wipes. "Grown-ups can use these, too," she says.

DAY 10: We're all sick of sandwiches on paper plates. We go to restaurant and pay $97 to eat steak on paper plates.

DAY 11: Friends from the next town invite us to their house for dinner and a shower. The kids are happy, but cautious. "Can we flush the toilet? Can we turn on the faucets? Is the water safe to drink? Does it have disease in it?"

DAY 12: We have water! We still can't drink it or shower in it but we can flush it. School's in session. Things are returning to normal, but the flood has left its high water mark on us. The kids now understand the meaning of community. They've donated blankets and toys to the Red Cross. They realize that two small children *can* make a difference and have started a fund to save our park. And they'll never, ever drink a cool, clean glass of water and take it for granted again.

Bye Bye, Blankie

Whenever Dash has Spencer spend the night, Spencer usually packs in about ten pounds worth of equipment. He brings a sleeping bag, pillow, several action figures, a couple of board games that he has created himself, AND . . . this dirty, matted hunk of fur that looks like a cross between a bathmat and road kill.

That dirty, matted hunk of fur is Spencer's "Lambie." I understand from Spencer's mom that Lambie used to be a large piece of lambskin. It's been with Spencer from the day he was first placed in his cradle. Lambie is Spencer's security blanket. Nine-year-old Spencer is not embarrassed about bringing Lambie to sleepovers because Dash has Huggy.

Huggy is a stuffed bear. Huggy used to be white and he used to have eyes. Once, during a cross-country trip, we accidentally left Huggy at a motel in Fargo, North Dakota. It was a huge crisis, and Malcolm and I moved heaven and earth to find Huggy and have him returned to us.

Marie's daughter Lily has a blanket she calls her "Little Me." When Lily was a toddler she never went anywhere without her Little Me. It's been washed so many times that all that remains is a one foot square piece of material. Lily doesn't take her Little Me to the store or kindergarten anymore, but it still lives in a special place in her closet. Whenever Lily feels sad or lonely, she asks Marie for her Little Me. Lily sniffs it, rubs it against her cheek, and her Little Me makes the hurt go away.

Susan and Jack's son Chase recently lost his faithful stuffed friend. Snowball was left in the airport in Boston. They must have called the lost-and-found at Logan twenty-five times. Jack made the two-hour round-trip drive to the airport at least three times. But they never found the little white bear with the wire-rimmed glasses and plaid vest.

Chase, who is nine, seems to be handling the loss of his beloved Snowball pretty well. He decided that Snowball went on to help another little boy grow up.

Susan and Jack are the ones having difficulty dealing with Snowball's loss. Susan still bursts into tears talking about it. I think losing that bear puts a period on Chase's infancy. He's not a baby anymore.

As much as we want our kids to grow up and be independent, it's so hard to let our babies go. Which is why my mom has a hat box hidden in the back of her closet with two scraps of blue and pink satin from my blankie. And why Malcolm and I have reserved a special place in our cedar chest for Skye's tattered Kitty Cat Blankie and Dash's gray, balding Huggy Bear.

Goodnight, Mrs. Hillgartner, Wherever You Are

Last week Malcolm's mother passed away. Rosie had battled cancer, diabetes, and heart disease for years and finally gave up the fight. Fortunately, Malcolm was able to spend time with her before she died. He was with her when she slipped away in her sleep.

The death of a parent is a difficult milestone. On one hand, you're frightened to be left alone in the world, with no back-up. On the other hand, it is the moment when the torch is passed and you truly become the parent.

Malcolm grieved for his loss, but worried as much about how our children, Dash and Skye, would handle the news of their grandma's death. Since he was gone it was up to me to tell them. But how? Just announcing, "Your grandma died," seemed to be so hollow. Death is huge. Enormous. It requires something that acknowledges that fact.

There are ceremonies for marriages, births, graduations. It seemed only fitting to Dash and Skye that we should have a ceremony for Grandma Rosie's death. The two of them planned the whole event.

That evening, they arranged their favorite pictures of Grandma Rosie in the center of the coffee table in the living room. Then they placed three candlesticks on the floor in front of the fireplace. Dash turned off all of the lights and gave us our instructions. One by one, we were to walk to the fireplace, pick up our candlestick, then carry it to the table and light it. Since Skye was the youngest, she was to go first.

Skye carefully carried her candlestick across the room and lit it. Her face aglow in the candle's light, Skye told us how she had loved Grandma Rosie since she was a little baby and that she was really going to miss her.

Dash took his turn, solemnly lighting his candle. He shared his favorite memories of Grandma, adding, "though she could sometimes be grumpy, she took us to the funnest parks and always gave us great stuffed animals."

When we'd all had our turn, the three of us huddled together on the couch in the candlelight. We hugged each other and cried for Malcolm, who would miss his mom. We cried for our family, who would miss our grandmother. And then, in hushed tones, the children told me that Grandma was now a part of the earth. She was in the wind, the flowers, the trees, and sky. Grandma was watching over us and smiling.

At the end of the ceremony, Dash played "Amazing Grace" on his flute. We blew out our candles and walked up the stairs holding hands. I wish Malcolm could have been there in body, but he was with us in spirit. And so was Grandma Rosie.

Nightmare on Oak Street

Malcolm and I write books for a living. Specifically books for eight- to twelve-year-olds and teens. As Jahnna N. Malcolm, we've written about ballerinas, horses, rebel angels, singing cowgirls, and green slime. A few years ago we jumped on the "scary book" wagon and added ghosts and monstrous creatures to that list.

The rules of writing scary books for young readers are pretty clear. No kid can ever die. A monster or two can be vaporized, but in general you try to keep murder out of your story. But we all know there are scarier things than death—like "ghosties, and ghoulies, and long-leggedy beasties, and things that go bump in the night."

We weren't really aware of the impact these stories could have on kids until we had two of our own.

When Dash was little he had normal kid nightmares and normal kid fears. He was worried about what might be under his bed at night and was not too keen about that space between the wall and his bed. Sometimes his toys took on odd shapes in the half-light. An open closet door could send him scurrying into our room. But it's Skye who had the whoppers.

From the time Skye could barely talk, she had nightmares about Owl and Pooh stealing her bottle. Shortly after she turned three, she called me to her room. "Mommy! I had a nightmare! It was called, 'The Cave.'" The next week she said, "I had a funny dream. It was called, 'The Pumpkinhead.'" I think the weirdest title she ever came up with was the nightmare she named, "Seekers of Darkness." (All this from a three-year-old.)

When Skye was four and Dash was almost seven, we were hired to ghostwrite a scary book for a well-known children's author. Since the language was simple and the chapters short, I decided I'd try out a few chapters on the kids while they were in the bathtub. Big mistake.

As I got to the part describing how a shadow monster on the wall became real, Dash shouted, "Stop! How could you write that? That's terrible!" For weeks I couldn't even mention the word "shadow" without sending him into a panic. But once again, it was Skye who was affected the most.

One night I heard a faint cry for help. When I went into her room, I found Skye buried under her covers. "Turn on the light, will you, Mom?" a muffled voice asked. "I'm just a little bit scared of the shadows." I turned on the light and she peeked out. I said, "The only shadows I see are from the lights on the street."

"All except that big hairy one by the door," Skye replied. I groaned, "Oh, honey, that shadow is from our book." "Well, it went out of your book and into my dream," she said, "and now it's standing over there in the corner!"

The next day we told our publisher we were out of the scary book business. Our next project was our Jewel Kingdom book series. It's for six- to nine-year-olds and is about princesses, unicorns, and friendly dragons. No one ever dies. And if there is a shadow, it's only a fluffy white cloud passing overhead.

The Best Laid Plans

When the end of May approaches, it's time for us parents to start planning our summer trips. People without kids planned theirs when they were supposed to—in January. And so did the people whose kids are now teenagers. They looked at guidebooks, talked to travel agents, made reservations, and mail-ordered the appropriate summer wear for their vacation.

But we of the terminally tired, terminally late club can't manage to get it together to plan a night out, let alone a vacation.

We're always a step behind. When I gave birth to Dash, we hadn't bought our crib, changing table, or even a pack of diapers. We wished we'd planned ahead, and vowed to do better the next time around. But new surprises hit us at every turn.

Nobody told us it would take forty-five minutes to pack a diaper bag and put a baby in traveling gear just to take a thirty-minute trip to the grocery store. That is something we learned to plan for, after the zillionth time we were late for doctor's appointments, dinner reservations, and play dates.

We had no idea a trip to a restaurant would mean packing a U-Haul of toys, coloring books, and surprise activities, just so you could make it through a meal. That's an extra hour that has to be built into your evening plans.

And speaking of planning, why didn't someone tell us you have to register for preschool before your baby is born? We thought you just showed up in August the year he turned three, put your name on a list, and by September your child was happily studying calculus and Greek.

As for after-school activities, these have to be scheduled months in advance. Spring soccer sign-up is in the fall. Summer camp checks are due in winter. And you'll get a special rate for fall ballet lessons if you sign up before the summer deadline. It's mind-numbing.

Now our children have thrown another wrench in the works: their own plans. When Skye and Dash were tiny, we would just meet with parents we liked and the kids either played together or sat around throwing blocks at each other. But now, Skye and Dash have kids they want to visit. Kids who live in other towns and on ranches way out in the country. That adds another hour or two of driving, which means planning for a lot of time in the car, which means carrying an extra load of snacks and an extra change of clothing (because during all of that extra travel time, the weather could change).

I'm so tired of planning, I think this summer's vacation will be unplanned. We will just pack a semi with swimsuits, inner tubes, gas grills, floaties, slip-and-slides, sleeping bags, and insect repellant and drive to the back yard. Maybe we'll circle the block first, so the kids can fight on the way.

Mother's Day Resolutions

It's Mother's Day and boy do I feel guilty! I don't deserve flowers picked from the neighbor's yard and frozen waffles smothered in butter and syrup. I flunk the Mother-of-the-Year test on all fronts. I'm a frazzled grouch that yells, "Put on your shoes, get in the car, pick up your toys, and stop fighting!" every hour, on the hour.

Malcolm is the one who deserves the flowers and the waffles. He is kind, considerate, and even-tempered. Where my motto has sometimes been, "Don't get mad, get even," his has always been, "Count to ten, begin again." Malcolm has only lost it a few times. But he was provoked—Skye did the flamenco on his guitar and Dash and his friends crashed the hard disk on his computer.

Malcolm is the glue that holds our household together. If he didn't cook, do the wash, and pack lunches, the kids would arrive at school undernourished and naked, clutching empty Pokemon lunch boxes.

This week I made a stab at cooking. I said, "Malcolm, you rent a movie, I'll make the kids spaghetti." I made the pasta, then pulled a jar of spaghetti sauce out of the fridge. I poured it on the noodles and served it. The children took one bite, clutched their throats and shouted, "Water!" It turns out the tomato sauce was in the cupboard. The extra hot garlic salsa was in the fridge.

I realize that being a good mom doesn't mean I have to be a great housekeeper or cook. But having at least one of those skills would be a plus.

So what would make me a better mom? I decided to make a list of the things I could do on a daily basis that would warrant a few flowers and a freezer-burned waffle:

1. Spend at least half an hour each day listening to the kids. This means just sitting and not doing anything else but hearing their words.

2. Spend another half hour reading to them or having them read to me.

3. Speaking of reading, take the kids to the library on a regular basis.

4. Instead of just shouting, "Turn off the TV!" offer them an alternative like playing a board game or doing a puzzle with me.

5. For every time I yell at the kids, praise them ten times.

6. When the kids ask me to play ball with them, say yes.

7. Don't always bark orders. As often as possible, let the kids make decisions and have choices.

8. Walk the poor dogs. (I'm their mother too.)

9. Try to remember not to sweat the small stuff.

10. Try to remember—it's all small stuff.

Gross Out!

In the course of raising our children, Malcolm and I have discovered that desperate times do indeed call for desperate measures!

It's hot. The kids are fighting in the backseat of the car. We've begged, we've threatened, we've wept, but they won't stop bickering. What do we do? Start looking for road kill.

The next dead possum, squirrel, or snake we see—we pull over. "Omigod, kids, look! That frog is flat as a pancake! He must have been mowed down by a semi!"

The fighting stops. The kids are hypnotized by the sight. And for the next half hour, we have peace as they discuss (in awed voices) how that poor frog came to such a sad end.

On the road kill front, I advise that it not be too fresh. We try to find something so dried up it's almost unrecognizable. That adds an element of "What do you think that was?" to their discussion.

The gross-out technique is really useful. It stops fights, dries tears, and gets your children's attention right now (something that's increasingly harder to do, we've discovered).

Once, during a long car trip in February, Malcolm and I promised the kids we would get a motel with a pool. After driving around some snow-choked town in eastern Washington for two hours, we finally found one. Its pool was indoors, heated, and open! We checked in, raced to our room, and threw on our swimsuits.

But a note was taped to the pool door: "Sorry, temporarily closed." The wail from our kids could be heard all the way back to Montana. I stormed to the front desk. "The only reason we registered here is because you swore you had a pool we could swim in—now." The clerk blushed and said, "Sorry. A kid just vomited in the water and all over the deck." Disgusting.

Hmm. . . . Maybe I could turn this to our advantage. I rushed back to my weeping children, who were still in their Mickey Mouse floaties. "Kids! You won't believe what happened. Some kid barfed in the pool. Do you want to go see it?"

Their tears vanished. Great green globs of floating barf were far more interesting than a dip in a pool. We hurried over and peered in the window. "I see it! Ew, gross!" We spent the rest of that evening wondering how the motel was going to get that barf out of the water.

One morning, I couldn't get the kids to wake up. I tried everything—shaking them, flicking the lights, and blasting them with loud music. Then I noticed our fuzzy dog, Clarence, had poop tangled in his fur. "Kids! You won't believe what's stuck to Clarence's bottom. . . ." They were up, dressed, and ready to cringe.

At this moment, there's a rack of peeling, rotting antlers in our garage. Dash insisted on bringing them home from a reindeer farm last December. They smelled when we got them, but now that it's warm, those decaying antlers are probably attracting all kinds of creepy crawlies. But are we going to throw them out? No way! We're saving them for the gross-out of the century!

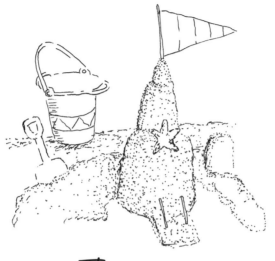

Less Is Less

I know we vowed to stay home this year, but the ad was irresistible. "Secluded Island Getaway!" and "Sun, sand, and surf!" it read. Malcolm and I decided to splurge. We bought four plane tickets and rented a house on Martha's Vineyard for August.

All July, visions of vacation heaven danced in our heads: Malcolm and I reclining in our beach chairs, cool drinks in our hands, with Dash and Skye quietly building sandcastles nearby. As our departure approached, we stuffed beach towels, bathing suits, sunscreen, and bug spray into suitcases. We couldn't wait to get to our Secluded Island Getaway.

It's now Day Four of our vacation. The cottage we rented is secluded. It sits in the woods at the end of a long, winding dirt road. It is a modern, light-filled home filled with expensive Art Deco furnishings. The couches are white, the dishes Fiestaware.

We promptly gave Dash and Skye strict orders not to play with or touch anything in this house. "If it breaks, we'll have to spend the rest of our lives paying for it." We told them not to sit on the white couches and to be careful of the wood floors. In fact, we told them, "Whenever possible, stay outside."

Our Secluded Island Getaway has its own private beach at the end of a long, winding path. But do the kids go there? No. Why? Because there aren't any kids on that beach. There don't seem to be kids anywhere near us.

For three days now, we've gotten up early and left our Secluded Island Getaway. We pile the children in the car and drive around the island looking for kids. On Monday, we found a few at a school playground, and a lot more at the public beach. Yesterday, we saw kids at the Flying Horse Carousel and the ice cream parlor, but we didn't talk to them. They already had friends. Friends who are staying in the crowded motel in Oak Bluffs.

Every day when we return to our expensive Secluded Island Getaway, the children want us to entertain them. Do we get to read novels? No. Do we get to veg out and soak up rays on our private beach? Of course not. We're too busy scouring the newspaper for kids' events, or yelling at the children, "Stop fighting. We're going to find some more kids, just give us a minute, will you?"

So what have we learned from this? We've learned that families don't need a Secluded Island Getaway. Those are for couples without kids. What we need is a Crowded Island Get-Together.

We should have signed up for one of those all-inclusive "room plus meals and daily kids' activities" packages. Like a Club Med vacation in Martinique. Or a Rascals in Paradise trip to Costa Rica. Or five nights at the Holiday Inn in Anywhere, USA.

Then we'd be spending the day lying by the pool and reading our books. We'd probably even meet a few frazzled parents like ourselves. While our kids dismantled the video game room, we'd sip our cocktails and compare "kids fighting in the car" stories. Our children would speak to us only when they needed quarters for the vending machines. And at night we'd take that short walk back to our rooms and veg out in front of a large screen TV. Heaven.

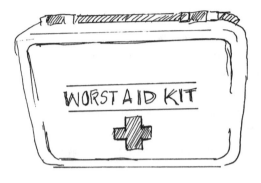

Worst Aid

For nine months out of the year, Malcolm and I are just parents willing to let the medical experts handle our kids' daily ills. But the second school lets out, we become the experts.

Armed with a first-aid kit stocked with antibiotic creams, Day-Glo Band-Aids, pain-relieving sprays, calamine lotion, and burn cream, we dispense medicine like candy. And we don't limit ourselves to over-the-counter products. In a pinch, we'll make our own home remedies. Home remedies can be found on your laundry room shelf, under your bathroom sink, or in your kitchen's spice rack.

When Dash was stung by a bee, I raced to the kitchen to make a paste of baking "something" (I couldn't remember if it was baking soda or baking powder, so I used both). "Forget the baking soda," Malcolm said, "what Dash needs is meat tenderizer. It's loaded with alum." While Malcolm was basting Dash with Adolph's, I remembered that our pediatrician once told us ammonia was the best remedy for a bee sting. So I doused Dash with a bottle of pine-scented Mr. Clean.

Our friend, Leslie, watched in horror as we smothered our son with floor cleaner, baking soda, and meat tenderizer. Afterward she said, "You're lucky Dash didn't explode!"

Tuesday, I found a dreaded deer tick on Skye's shoulder blade. Remembering that deer ticks carry Lyme disease, I wanted that creature off my baby—NOW!

I'd heard you should drown ticks in mineral oil. But I didn't have any. I did have mineral oil-based bug repellent. So I blasted Skye's shoulder with a quart of bug spray. It smelled like rotting lemons. Then, just to be safe, I poured half a bottle of olive oil down her back, which made her smell like a Caesar salad with extra anchovies. Once I'd removed the tick with tweezers, I covered Skye in hydrogen peroxide and triple-antibiotic cream. By the time I was finished, she smelled like a dumpster behind an Italian restaurant.

With summer almost over and our first-aid kits running low on supplies, you'd think we'd back off on the "annihilate a bug bite" philosophy. But noooooooooo.

Last night the kids wanted to go for a bike ride in our mosquito-infested woods with their friend, Chase. No way were we going to let them set foot in those woods unprotected.

I rubbed each child's arms, legs, and neck with a citronella wipette. Chase's mom, Susan, rushed into the kitchen to whip up her own home remedy of eucalyptus oil bug repellent. In the meantime, Malcolm found a sixteen-ounce can of Deep Woods Off! and hosed them down with it. As the kids rode off on their bikes, Malcolm read the warning label out loud: "Avoid contact with eyes and lips. Do not allow children to rub eyes. Do not apply to excessively sunburned skin. Keep treated surfaces away from fire or flame. Hazardous to humans."

We realized the kids were wearing enough chemicals on their bodies to be declared a toxic waste site. "Look on the bright side," Susan said. "At least cars will be able to see them. They glow in the dark."

Star Soup

One of the last nights of summer I happened to be up at three in the morning. Skye had a nightmare and Dash wanted a glass of water. Ruby the dog, seeing all the commotion, wanted to go out. After everyone went back to sleep, I couldn't. So I went to the bedroom window and, quite by accident, looked up.

A flash of light like something out of a sci-fi movie blazed across the sky. Seconds later, two more meteors shot across the stars. Then came still more. I soon realized that I'd blundered onto the Perseid meteor shower, an annual bonanza known only to astronomers and insomniacs.

I woke Malcolm, and the two of us stood on the deck and watched the shooting stars. It was like the Fourth of July, only better. Soon Dash wandered downstairs and joined us. He got chilled, so we wrapped him in a blanket. The three of us watched the firework display for a long time.

When it became clear that this was no teaser but a full-blown production, we knew we'd better wake Skye, or she'd never forgive us for leaving her out.

We pulled a mattress onto the deck and all of us lay on our backs, snuggled under down comforters, watching the stars. We spotted Jupiter and the Pleiades. The kids found their own constellations: "That's the Pancake Turner constellation." "Look over there, that's the Doghouse."

And all the while, meteors of different colors whizzed over-head. Some were "streakers," brief spurts of light that barely appeared before vanishing. Others were "flamers," great bursts of orange light, with comet-like tails. Dash informed us that they were very fast spaceships traveling from one star to another. Skye declared we were watching "star soup."

The four of us lay side by side, experiencing something more wonderful than Disneyland, the waterslides, carnival rides, or anything we've ever paid for. The kids spoke in hushed tones, feeling the importance of this magnificent event.

As I lay there, I realized it had been an awfully long time since I had just looked up. And it had been an awfully long time since I'd really listened to our children. No one had to be the parent and tell anyone to do anything. We were just four kids enjoying the wonder of the universe.

We watched the stars until they blinked out with the dawn. As we finally drifted off to sleep, Malcolm murmured, "You know? It doesn't get any better than this."

Boo Who?

---

remember the exact moment I gave up trying to win the Betty Crocker Homemaker Award. It was October 31, 1991. Halloween. Dash had just started preschool. I was nine months pregnant and looked like the Great Pumpkin.

Dash's teacher asked for volunteers to bake treats for their Halloween party. I had never baked in my entire life. But I figured, "Of course I can bake. I'm a mom. Baking is what moms do best."

Visions of dainty cupcakes with little ghosts and witches danced in my head. I bought a cupcake pan, mix, white frosting, food coloring, and squeeze tubes of black gel.

But when it came time to bake, I discovered I'd bought banana muffin mix instead of cupcake mix. Before I got too weepy, Malcolm convinced me that muffins would be much healthier than sugary old cupcakes.

Malcolm baked the muffins and early the next morning, I decorated them. But I had a little trouble making the orange frosting. The stuff I plastered on the muffins was a sickly yellow sludge with thick red glops.

Malcolm assured me that the witch and ghost designs would cover the glops. But they didn't cover them—they joined them! Shaky lines of black gel oozed all over the red and yellow glops.

In a panic, I covered the black smears with rock hard **raisins**. Disgusting. I yanked the raisins off the muffins, leaving gaping holes in the frosting. You could no longer tell what the black smears with the potholes were supposed to be. I cried.

Malcolm shooed me out of the kitchen promising he'd fix things. I hurried to help Dash get into his dinosaur costume, while Malcolm filled the holes with chocolate chips.

Dash's dinosaur costume was a pair of cute green dino pajamas with a spiked hood and tail that I had duct-taped and pinned together. Dash loved it. He paraded around in a circle roaring. I cried again, this time for joy. (Remember I was nearly ten months pregnant.)

Malcolm set the muffins on the back seat next to Dinosaur Dash, hoisted me into the front seat and we headed for school. When we arrived, we discovered that Dash had not only eaten every single chocolate chip off the muffins, but he'd made his own designs in the frosting.

I carried my miserable tray of mutilated muffins into the school and froze. Not two feet in front of me was Katie

Parker's mother, with her tray. It was covered with two dozen of the prettiest orange frosted cupcakes you've ever seen. Flying atop each cupcake with was a perfectly drawn witch on a broomstick.

A bloodcurdling scream filled the air.

No, it wasn't me. It was Dash. He had just seen Spencer Reynolds in his perfect white rabbit costume. "I want to be a bunny!" Dash wailed, pulling at his duct-taped dinosaur tail. "Get this thing off me."

The rest of the party is a blur. I remember hiding my muffins in the storage room. I remember finally getting Dash to stop crying. And then I remember my trip to the hospital.

The next morning I gave birth to our daughter, Skye Mckenna.

Now, whenever a teacher calls and asks me to bake something, Malcolm quickly grabs the phone (before I can go into labor) and says, "You can count on us. We'll be bringing two dozen cookies from our favorite baker, Safeway."

skye

Who Put the Magic in Markers?

I have two words of advice for grandparents: washable markers. I'm targeting grandparents because they're the ones who give our kids those spiffy "everything-you'll-ever-need-to-make-a-permanent-artistic-statement" kits.

These kits are great. Sometimes they come in the shape of a puppy or a kitty. Or they look like miniature dressers decorated in Jungle Safari or Under the Sea contact paper. No matter what's on the outside, I guarantee that inside that spiffy box lurks an indelible marker.

Dash's first Young Painter kit from Grandma Rosie included a vivid green marker. Now, these kits never come with blank paper, but even if they did—who needs paper when you've got that heirloom cedar chest at the foot of Mommy and Daddy's bed? Looking at that green snake drawing still makes me wince.

You can track our kids' growth by the stuff scrawled on the walls and cupboards. I'm sure the people who bought our log home in Montana were thrilled to discover that red stripe circling the living room about two feet above the floor. We never noticed it until we were moving out. But I can tell you who did it—little baby Skye with her Pretty Kitty paint kit. It included crayons, pastels, watercolors, and . . . a bright red NON-washable Magic Marker. Delivered into her tiny hands by none other than Aunt Debbie.

Last summer Malcolm and I had a rip-snorting argument over a lamp. It cost a lot of money eight years ago, but it didn't go with our new house at all. So it was tucked away in a closet. I wanted to sell it at a garage sale. He was appalled. "How can you throw away a perfectly good, expensive lamp?" I finally convinced him that just because you spent a lot of money on something once doesn't mean you have to live with it for the rest of your life.

Malcolm reluctantly agreed to let me sell it for $50. Well, when I got out the lamp, the harsh light of day revealed that once upon a time a tiny hand had scribbled up and down the base with a thin blue marker. It looked like an EKG. We had to beg someone to take it off our hands for the price of the light bulb.

After Skye wrote her name with a backwards "k" on every doorsill in the house, I declared war on non-washable markers. Any relative entering the house had to be frisked. That worked until last week, when I broke my own rule and bought three black Magic Markers to draw designs on our Halloween pumpkins.

Our darling daughter drew a design, all right. In the center of the dining room table. She wanted to see what it looked like first, before she drew on her pumpkin. I know what you're thinking: so why didn't she use a piece of paper?

That's the question that wakes me up at three in the morning. I don't come up with any answers—only more questions. Like why would she empty an entire bottle of shampoo into the bathtub the day I bought it? And why would she wipe her bottom with the guest towels, and put them back on the rack? And why, oh, WHY would she take a paper clip and etch-a-sketch a three-foot tall butterfly on the sliding door of our new van?

$\mathcal{S}$urprise Packages

Two weeks ago, Skye came to us and said in the most angelic voice: "The absolute only thing I want for Christmas is a little baby kitten."

Our family has Ruby, a big golden retriever, and Clarence, a medium-sized shaggy mutt. Both of our dogs were strays who showed up on our doorstep. So Malcolm cleverly told Skye, "All of our pets find us. If a kitten comes to us looking for a home this Christmas, then, yes, you can have a kitty."

Now I ask you, what are the odds of that happening?

The very next day, I'm walking Skye to preschool and who should come bounding onto the sidewalk but a big mamma cat and two little kittens. Seconds later, a car pulls up beside us and the driver says, "Those cats just appeared on my doorstep last night. Do you know of anyone who would like a kitten?" Skye turns to me and announces, "I'll take the little black one with the white whiskers."

I have to admit, it was too much of a Twilight Zone moment for me to say a firm no. I told Skye we'd talk it over with Daddy. When we told Malcolm what had happened, he shrugged helplessly. "It's fate," he declared. "We have to let her have that kitten."

We couldn't just leave the little black kitten with the white whiskers on that lady's doorstep until Christmas. We took it home. We also took the Siamese one home for Dash. (The lady kept the mamma cat for herself.)

Sam and Whiskers have been with us for a week now. The house smells like a catbox. The kittens have given our dogs fleas. When they aren't scratching, Ruby and Clarence run frantically around the house panting and barking at the kittens, who spend a lot of time knocking ornaments and tinsel off the Christmas tree. At night the kitties wait until I'm just about to fall asleep, then sneak up on the bed and bite my nose.

But that's small potatoes compared to what we discovered yesterday. We were standing in a packed line waiting to see Santa at the mall's North Pole Village, when Dash held up his arm and cried, "Mom, look at this red circle, Do you think I have cancer?" "Of course not," I replied firmly. "That's ringworm. I'm sure of it." Five parents and two elves instantly flattened themselves against Santa's sleigh as I examined Skye, who also had ringworm, and Malcolm, who didn't. Now Dash's friend Chase has ringworm. So does Skye's best friend, Katie. I've taken to enclosing anti-fungal cream in all of our Christmas presents.

So if any of you were thinking of dropping by our house this holiday season—don't. Just drive on by. And take Santa and his mangy beasts with you. There's no room at this inn.

Seeing Is Believing

One day in fourth grade, my teacher asked, "How many of you believe in Santa Claus?"

I was the only kid who raised her hand. Everyone laughed. To make matters worse, Mrs. Solomon asked me to come sit on a chair at the front of the class while she read us Francis P. Church's famous editorial, "Yes, Virginia, There Is a Santa Claus."

I think if Mrs. Solomon had asked, "How many of you want to believe in Santa Claus?" more kids would have raised their hands.

All of us want to believe in magic. My brother and I pretended we believed in Santa until we were almost in junior high. My parents wanted us to believe, we wanted to believe, so we believed.

Last year, Dash's friends were telling him there was no Santa. He asked me point-blank, "Mom? Is there a Santa Claus?" I've discovered with big questions like, "Is there a Santa Claus?" and, "Who is God?" it's always better to answer with the question, "What do you think?" Generally kids give the answer they want to hear.

On the "Is there a God?" question, Skye said, "God is a man and a woman who watches over us." Dash said, "God isn't a person. God is the sky and earth and trees." According to my friend's daughter Lily, "God is the luckiest guy in town. He gets all the balloons."

When I asked Dash what he thought about Santa, he paused and said very carefully, "I think Santa only comes to the homes of children who believe in him." Good answer.

Malcolm and I love Santa. It's one of the perks of being a parent. You get to have Santa, the Easter Bunny, the Tooth Fairy, and Halloween all over again. We're in no hurry to give up all that magic.

Every now and then you meet some adult who tells a sad story about the day he found out there was no Santa, and how he still feels betrayed that his parents lied to him when he was a kid. Those are the adults who won't allow any magic into their own children's lives. And their children are the ones in preschool announcing to one and all that there is no Santa because, "my daddy says so."

I feel sorry for those adults and their kids, but Malcolm and I are standing firm about believing in magic. Because it's the magic in this world that makes miracles happen.

And December is the time of year when we all celebrate miracles. Like the miracle of one small lamp that burned for eight days and nights, lighting the darkness with hope and faith. Or the birth of one tiny baby who changed the world.

Head 'em Up, Move 'em Out!

I'm writing this from inside a bunker of packing boxes. We just moved and I can't find a thing. I spent all morning circling the house searching for my car keys, the kids' shoes, and the cat. Every time I need a pen, I grab this wooden chopstick. What are we doing with one chopstick? And why is it the only thing that is unpacked? When I packed these boxes, I was very careful to label them with their contents and what room they belonged in. However, we borrowed these boxes from M. McLaughlin, who was also very careful to label her boxes with their contents and designated room. And to make matters even more complicated, she got those boxes from S.R. Stewart, who did her own labeling.

Six years ago, when we told Dash we were moving to Oregon, he said, "Okay," and disappeared into his room. Ten minutes later he reappeared with a bag full of Legos and stuffed animals, and said, "I'm ready." This time wasn't so easy—especially with Skye. "I was born in this house!" she wailed every time we mentioned selling it. She wasn't, but it's the only home she remembers.

Skye has always had difficulty with change. When we got a new washer, she cried, "How could you get rid of our washer?" "It didn't work," we replied. "But it washed my clothes just fine," she announced firmly. When we sold our old couch and bought a new one, she stubbornly refused to sit on it for nearly a month.

Of course we knew leaving our home was going much different than losing a couch or an old washer. We did everything we could to prepare the kids for the big move but when moving day finally came, there we were, trucks loaded, pets in the car, engines running, and no Skye. I went upstairs and found her huddled in the corner of her room, sobbing. We turned off the engines and took the time to really say good-bye to our home. Skye kissed every wall. The kids wrote their names on the same doorjamb where their heights had been measured. Then our family held hands in the empty living room and said, "We love you, old house. We'll never forget you."

Three days have now passed since we left the old place an moved six blocks across town. This afternoon, I personally handed the garbage man that chopstick to guarantee its removal from the premises. Skye still hasn't found her shoes but she's borrowed a pair of flip-flops from the neighbor girl. Oh, yeah. We found the cat. He was in the box labeled (in three different handwritings) Dishes—Kitchen, Pictures—Living Room, Stuffed Animals—Dash's Room. I still haven't found my mind. I suspect it's in that box labeled Miscellaneous–Garage.

For over twenty years, Jahnna Beecham and Malcolm Hillgartner have collaborated across a range of creative fields. Under the pen name Jahnna N. Malcolm, they have written over eighty books for young adults and children.

Additionally, they wrote weekly columns, "A Family Journal," featured on *Sesame Street Online*, and "The Jahnna and Malcolm Show," for *Sesame Street Parents* magazine.

Currently, the couple works as the editorial directors and creative writers for Gateway Learning Company, providing content for the "Hooked on School Success" interactive learning CD-ROM.

The parents of two school-aged children, Beecham and Hillgartner live in Ashland, Oregon.